"This story brings to life the unique men who form the ranks of the Green Berets and the Herculean tasks they must accomplish day in and day out, month after month, year after year."

—Rusty Bradley, author of *Lions of Kandahar*

"[A] powerful look at Special Forces and the daily grind of tracking down the Taliban, terrorists, and other bad guys in Afghanistan. Maurer . . . skillfully weaves it all into a compelling narrative."

—Mitch Weiss, Pulitzer Prize–winning journalist and critically acclaimed author of *Tiger Force* and *No Way Out*

"A true and refreshing narrative . . . Humorous, stark, and honest, *Gentlemen Bastards* shows the reality of the war in Afghanistan and proves that true, unbiased journalism is still alive."

—Nathan Edmondson, author of *The Activity*

"An authentic insider's account . . . This is a compelling book."

—David Zucchino, Pulitzer Prize winner and author of *Thunder Run*

"Maurer captures the humor of the Green Berets even while keeping his own self-deprecating, smart-ass-reporter-along-for-the-ride sensibility." —Kelly Kennedy, author of *They Fought for Each Other*

GENTLEMEN BASTARDS

On the Ground in Afghanistan with
America's Elite Special Forces

KEVIN MAURER

BERKLEY CALIBER, NEW YORK

THE BERKLEY PUBLISHING GROUP
Published by the Penguin Group
Penguin Group (USA) Inc.
375 Hudson Street, New York, New York 10014, USA

USA I Canada I UK I Ireland I Australia I New Zealand I India I South Africa I China

Penguin Books Ltd., Registered Offices: 80 Strand, London WC2R 0RL, England
For more information about the Penguin Group, visit penguin.com.

BERKLEY CALIBER and its logo are trademarks of Penguin Group (USA) Inc.

ISBN: 978-0-425-25359-5

The Library of Congress has catalogued the Berkley Caliber hardcover edition as follows:

Maurer, Kevin.
Gentlemen bastards : on the ground in Afghanistan with America's elite special forces / by Kevin Maurer.
p.   cm.
ISBN 978-0-425-25269-7 (alk. paper)
1. Afghan War, 2001—Commando operations.   2. Special operations (Military science)—Afghanistan.
3. Special operations (Military science)—United States.   I. Title.
DS371.412.M38   2012
658.104'742—dc23
2012005721

PUBLISHING HISTORY
Berkley Caliber hardcover edition: September 2012
Berkley Caliber trade paperback edition: June 2013

PRINTED IN THE UNITED STATES OF AMERICA

10 9 8 7 6 5 4 3 2 1

Cover design by George Long
Cover photos courtesy of Ben Watson
Book design by Laura K. Corless

War was always here. Before man was, war waited for him. The ultimate trade awaiting its ultimate practitioner.

—CORMAC McCARTHY,
Blood Meridian or the Evening Redness in the West

This was also the quote selected by Gregg, the team's senior medic, to write on the back of ODA 7316's team shirts.

GENTLEMEN
BASTARDS

CHAPTER 1

THE GREEN BERETS

You can tell a lot about a soldier just by looking at his body armor.

Climbing aboard the Shadow flight, a sort of private charter flown by the air force for the special operations community in Afghanistan, I scanned the other passengers. I could tell from their scruffy beards and worn gear how long the group of rail-thin Rangers had been in country. The other soldiers, a few Special Forces soldiers with equally worn gear, were mixed in with the staff soldiers who wore pristine and clean armor.

It was fall 2010. I was flying from Bagram, the large American base near Kabul, to Kandahar, the largest base in southern Afghanistan, to meet up with a Special Forces team I would embed with for the next ten weeks. Special Forces teams were playing an integral part of President Barack Obama's revamped strategy to surge thirty thousand additional troops into Afghanistan to destroy the Taliban and build a stable government.

The Rangers barely looked at me. To them, I was some civilian analyst or contractor. My body armor, for one thing, was clean, lacking any of the moon dust that coats everything in Afghanistan. Two, I didn't have any pouches needed to carry essential gear on patrols or raids. And finally, my beard was thin. I was a nobody, or worse, a "Fobbit," which is a derogatory term for those who live and work on the large bases.

I quickly found a spot on the floor, near the crew chief, and settled in for the flight. Unlike the way it was across the tarmac at the conventional side of the airport, there was no formality. You get on the manifest, meet the plane, and find a spot on the floor.

Big-boy rules.

Propping myself up against my backpack, I ran a hand through my thin whiskers, the starting point for my future beard, and glanced down at my pristine body armor. While I'd worn the gear on two trips previously, it lacked that battle-hardened look of the Rangers and Special Forces soldiers. I didn't have to look up to know the Rangers and other soldiers had already taken one look at me and made their assessment. I knew that in the eyes of the men around me, I was a cherry. A new guy who hadn't done anything yet.

That was true for this trip because only a few days before, I was flying out of Atlanta on my way to Bagram by way of Dubai. But in reality it was my thirteenth trip overseas to cover the war and my fifth trip with Special Forces. This time was different because I wasn't coming as a reporter. This time I was coming to write a book. And not any book. I'd somehow come up with this idea that I was the man to write a contemporary version of Robin Moore's *Green Berets*.

The latter book is the unofficial bible of the Special Forces. All of them have read it, can quote from it, and point to it as a source of inspiration. It also doesn't hurt that John Wayne turned it into a movie.

Moore, a civilian, is credited with giving Special Forces its nickname. Though they had worn a beret unofficially, it wasn't until a visit to Fort Bragg, North Carolina, by President John F. Kennedy in 1961 that the green beret was made the official headgear of the Army Special Forces. Moore's book made the unit's headgear more than just a hat. It became a household name. A symbol of the Army's most elite soldier.

Moore, author of several books and a classmate of JFK, got the first look at the new unit and became the first true embedded journalist by training with and fighting alongside the Green Berets in Vietnam. He recounted stories of Green Berets defending remote outposts, of a lone Green Beret who goes native to fight alongside tribesmen in Laos, and finally how the Green Berets recruited a beautiful Vietnamese woman and used her as bait to capture a Vietcong colonel. The fact-based novel reads like a thriller and created the Green Berets' reputation.

I've had the unique experience of living with and following Green Berets in combat. But I, myself, am not a Green Beret.

I am not even a soldier. The closest I've ever come to being in the military was three years of Naval ROTC at Old Dominion University in Norfolk, Virginia. But I quit in 1997 with one semester left. I'd just returned from my senior cruise around the Baltic Sea with stops in Northern Ireland, Norway, Russia, and Scotland on a frigate.

I loved the port calls. Drank way too much beer and still don't properly recall exactly how I got from the ship to the airport to go home. The times I spent with the officers and crew of the ship are still fond memories. But when I wasn't working, I was asking questions. A couple of times when I wanted to know why something was done a certain way, I was summarily told "it was the Navy way," which only left me to ask why again like a petulant two-year-old. And when I finally went to my rack in officer overflow—really just a hallway with bunks—I dreamed of larger staterooms. It was then that I was convinced I wasn't a warrior.

So, after bouncing around a few jobs in Washington, D.C., and starting my career in journalism in Boston as a music writer (free CDs and concert tickets), I got a staff job writing about OSHA, the Occupational Safety and Health Administration, back in D.C. There I learned how to be a reporter and talked my way on staff at the *Fayetteville Observer*. Mike Adams, then the assistant managing editor, gave me a shot covering the military.

Learning from longtime military editor Henry Cunningham, I studied the units, quickly learned the difference between a platoon and a brigade, and started to learn all the ranks. But it wasn't until one of my colleagues got engaged in Kuwait to an officer she had been covering that I got my chance to cover a war. I spent the next month following the 82nd Airborne Division's 2nd Brigade Combat Team as they worked their way from Kuwait to Baghdad. It was 2003, and after covering the invasion, I focused on getting an embed with Special Forces in Afghanistan.

It took me a year. But I got it. And in the fall of 2004, I went to southern Afghanistan to cover a 3rd Special Forces Group ODA. It was during that embed that I got to see the Green Berets in their natural habitat. I followed that up with three more embeds and a year-long project on the Special Forces qualification course before getting the chance to come over and write a book.

But I am no more a Green Beret than a researcher who spends months with gorillas in the wild is a gorilla. No, the title of Green Beret can only be earned after a rigorous selection process and months of intense training in culture, language, and specialty skills.

I think it is hard to argue with the statement that Special Forces are America's most elite soldiers. It is not because they can shoot the straightest, run the fastest, or do the most push-ups. What makes them special are their smarts. They are the smartest soldiers on the battlefield. They can beat you with a handshake after a long negotiation just as easily as with a bullet.

More than forty years since the Vietnam War, the Green Berets are in a similar position to the one they were in then. The United States is again at war, this time in Afghanistan, and the Green Berets are playing an even greater role than before. But while much of Moore's book was still relevant, especially the scenes that highlight the Green Berets' unconventional methods in Vietnam, much of it was ripe for a rewrite.

Afghanistan is the Green Berets' war. With the United States on the verge of cutting combat forces as a prelude to the eventual pullout, Special Forces teams and the Afghans they train are more important than ever before.

So my pitch was to do a sort of homage. After getting the Army's approval, I set off to follow in Moore's footsteps, hoping to write the second volume to his book. But what I'd find was a book about a different kind of Green Beret, fighting a different war.

No long, drawn-out battles.

No decisive raid that breaks the will of the enemy.

Instead, I got the inside story of life on a Special Forces team, warts and all. The boredom of chasing an elusive enemy, of managing third-world cops, of dealing with the infighting among teammates and other units, especially conventional officers who don't understand that a Special Forces team is best left alone to do its work.

I also learned how easy it is to lose objectivity. You see, I'd played the role of reporter before. So, with the book, I went all in. I wore the Afghan uniform on patrol. Carried extra ammo and worked side by side to build a Special Forces base. About the only thing I didn't do was carry a weapon.

But I considered it.

Nine years after the start of the Afghan war, I found a force pressed for time, searching for a new identity, and trying to salvage victory in a war that started off as the "good" fight.

CHAPTER 2

TRIBES

It seemed fitting that the featured movie on my fourteen-hour flight from Atlanta to Dubai was *The A-Team*.

Between naps on the floor of the Shadow flight, I couldn't stop thinking about the movie's dumb action perpetrated by a Special Forces team accused of a crime they didn't commit in Iraq. The movie featured some of the worst abuses of the Army uniform in history. The team wore 7th Special Forces Group beret flashes, but kept talking about their time in the Rangers.

The thing that struck me about the movie, despite the fact that it was silly at best and groan-inducing bad at worst, was that in some ways it highlighted what Special Forces do. Not destroying things, but thinking unconventionally. Nothing the A-team did in the movie was conventional. They never just ran up and shot the bad guys.

That would be too easy.

Instead, they rappelled down buildings, shot through windows, and swooped in with helicopters to capture a prisoner floating to earth in a parachute. All far-fetched, but the action sequences spoke to the fact that Special Forces soldiers find unconventional ways to perform a mission. They dress up in local native garb to mask their movements. They are willing to eat the nasty parts of a goat to win over a village elder and hold hands with Afghan cops who want to be friends.

Too often people get wrapped up in the popular *Rambo* narrative and forget that the Special Forces were created not to destroy things but to sneak behind enemy lines and turn civilians into a functioning army. Part warriors and part teachers, Special Forces teams must be able to fight with and build rapport among foreign soldiers, sometimes at the same time. They are among the Army's most highly trained soldiers, taught to think like guerrillas who might perform a raid at night and work closely with locals to undermine an insurgency the next morning.

Until the war in Iraq, Special Forces were the military's counterinsurgency experts. They spent years training foreign armies and toppled the Taliban by mentoring Northern Alliance fighters. But in the almost nine years since, Special Forces units have instead focused on raids. Now, with time running out in Afghanistan, Special Forces are once again going back to their roots and have started to focus on training Afghan security forces and building the Afghan government one village at a time.

It is a mission only the Special Forces can do. In a meeting with his generals, General Petraeus reportedly told his commanders that the Green Berets now have the lead in the war. Good timing for me. I was hoping to catch the end of the summer fighting season and be around for the elections. I expected a big push in the fall to rid the south of the Taliban before winter set in and the fighters rested in Pakistan.

My goal was to take readers on a travelogue into the world of Special Forces in Afghanistan. Imagine the Green Berets as a tribe and the battlefield as their native habitat. Like a tribe, they will have common traits, attitudes, and beliefs. Their society operates under the same rules (big-boy rules), and they worship under the type A mantra of can-do attitudes and an unwavering sense that they can not only train anyone to be a soldier, but can build rapport with the youngest Afghan as well as the oldest.

But it was also a chance for me to scratch my adventure itch. After months of working a normal job and coming home to a normal house and normal family, I wanted to get to play Indiana Jones. There is nothing like going overseas. With each mile from the United States, the stress of daily life melts away.

No more cell phones.

No more e-mail.

And this time no daily deadlines. For this project, I had a chance to really dig into the team and not get up every day concerned if I had a story or not. For this one, I was going to try to live with the tribe.

And Special Forces is a tribe of brothers in the truest sense. They pick on each other without mercy, but not out of hate. Out of the fact that at some point they are going to need each other to survive, because unlike conventional units, their family is fewer than twenty guys.

The Shadow flight didn't get me to Kandahar until early the next morning. Dumping those of us headed to the Special Forces base at a far-off slab of tarmac across the runway from the terminal, we waited until the C-130 taxied away before piling into trucks and headed to Camp Brown. There, I met Sergeant Ben Watson.

Watson was my public affairs escort. We'd be stuck together for the next ten weeks and he'd quickly become my partner more than minder. Part philosopher and a better writer than I am, he became invaluable to the project. We'd talk writing. Do interviews together and stand countless hours in the back of an armored truck or walk side by side for miles on patrol.

A devoted fan of David Foster Wallace, he and I quickly developed a good partnership over books—his tastes far more refined than my own—both in music and movies.

But at 4 A.M. on that first day, all I wanted was a bed.

The center of Camp Brown, named after Sergeant First Class Bill Brown, was the latrines. The white building sat on the main drag into the camp and was an easy landmark.

Unloading my backpack and kit bag—a large green duffel bag—from the truck, I met Ben on the steps. With an American Spirit cigarette dangling from his mouth, he looked surprised to see me. Since he had no idea if I'd made the flight, he was just working up a note with the code to the VIP sleeping quarters and other information for me. Both of us were too tired for a lot of small talk. So, with little fanfare, he marched me over to the room near the headquarters and left me there to sleep off the jet lag.

The VIP quarters were VIP in name only, but for me, any bed would do. A small room with two bunk beds, a few chairs, and a table. But the VIP part was the Internet connection for sure. By the time I got into the room, though, I was too tired to care. I was soon fast asleep, but after a few hours I woke in a familiar place.

I'd been to Camp Brown many times in the past. In 2004, I'd been at the camp for a few days before working my way out to a team. At that time the war was considered "forgotten" and the teams had autonomy to do what needed to be done. There were few restrictions. Teams basically got an area to operate in and were given a simple mission: disrupt Taliban operations in that area.

The Taliban took control of Afghanistan in 1996 with the aim of creating a pure Islamic state. After decades of fighting and corruption, many Afghans welcomed the Taliban as the country's best chance for peace.

But the Taliban turned out to be oppressive, banning music, television, and movies. Women and girls were forced out of jobs and schools and into all-concealing burkas. Sharia, or Islamic law, was enforced in the form of public executions.

The Taliban also had a houseguest—Osama bin Laden. The al-Qaeda leader first fought the Soviets in Afghanistan in the 1980s. Once the Red Army left, he began using Afghanistan as a training ground for terrorists. In 2001, the country was the safe haven from which the attacks on the World Trade Center and the Pentagon were launched.

The American response to those attacks destroyed the Taliban as a political force in Afghanistan. Special Forces soldiers and a collection of anti-Taliban groups called the Northern Alliance routed the regime in a matter of months.

Some of the Taliban fighters and their leaders fled to Pakistan. But some stayed in Afghanistan and are counting on blending back into the population.

I'd dreamed of going to Afghanistan since September 2001. From the start of the war, I'd been determined to get a job covering it.

Living in Washington, D.C., at the time, I was less than a mile from the Pentagon when it got hit. My first embeds took me to Iraq for the invasion and the start of the insurgency. I wouldn't make it to Afghanistan until 2004.

The war in Afghanistan then was what I'd always envisioned the war in Vietnam to have been like. There were few restrictions even for reporters. The embed process didn't take weeks. All you had to do was find a unit that was willing to take you along.

My first embed with Special Forces was amazing. Meeting up

with a seasoned team, I was taken along as they tracked down a Taliban commander near Tarin Kowt. They did it using a motley collection of Afghan fighters, mostly Hazaras who fought against the Taliban. They'd gotten intelligence that the commander was using a phone in a nearby village. With no idea what the commander looked like, they went to the village hoping to find the phone.

On the way, one of their Afghans rolled a truck, causing the team to make adjustments on the fly. Cross-loading the other trucks, they changed the plan and still successfully hit the village. The commander wasn't there, but eventually wandered into the village and was caught.

When I'd left in 2004, the captain told me that the Taliban had a few more months left before they'd fold. He said the Special Forces had reduced the movement into survival of the fittest with the war turning into a gang fight.

"*The Sopranos* in man jammies" is what the team sergeant called it.

But the war had changed since 2004. After years of neglect in favor of Iraq, Afghanistan now became the main effort. The elections had brought it to the forefront and President Obama's presidential campaign made a point of promising more success in Afghanistan, a battleground known for swallowing empires.

I'd returned a few years later in 2007 and sat in a firebase with a Special Forces team after the country's first parliamentary elections. And I'd come back in 2009, but by then the war had really changed. The Obama administration had sent in a surge of troops—thirty thousand more soldiers and Marines—in an effort to keep the pressure on the Taliban.

The added emphasis had made the embed process long and detailed. Moving among units was nearly impossible without approval and the missions themselves were even different. It took weeks, not hours, to plan and execute them. Even the simple missions needed approval from multiple commanders and raids took at least a week to get all the levels to sign off.

But in 2009, the Special Forces had started Village Stability Operations. Essentially, teams were living and working in villages in hopes of creating a stable local government and police force. Special Forces units in Afghanistan were drastically expanding a program of putting units in rural villages to make it harder for Taliban and other insurgent groups to find a safe haven.

"We're going to kill the enemy, but that is not how we're going to win," Colonel Don Bolduc, commander of the Combined Joint Special Operations Task Force in Afghanistan, had told me before I arrived. "This is about mobilizing the populace. We're going to win by securing the populace and preventing the insurgents' negative influence."

The program sought to empower tribal leaders to keep insurgents out and linked the leaders to the government in Kabul. The villages were then given reconstruction projects and other support that they could take back to their tribes. This type of program was successful in Iraq, especially in the Anbar Province, where tribal leaders created councils that helped push insurgents out of the area. The designers, whom I spoke with in 2009, thought a similar effort would work in Afghanistan. They said Afghans traditionally distrust any central government and forcing them to recognize a Western-style government based in Kabul was not working.

"The important thing is that it is bottom up," said one of the program managers.

The program is a departure from the raid-based missions that were common in the early years of the war and experts say that it leverages the strengths of Special Forces. It was exactly what Special

Forces should have been doing throughout the war, and I was hoping to see a team carry it out firsthand.

Still half asleep and fighting jet lag, I waited to get out to a village in the northern part of Kandahar Province. But as with anything in the Army, it took time to arrange everything. So while Ben and Staff Sergeant Jeremy Crisp worked up a plan, I waited.

Things seemed different from the year before. There was a manic energy. It was like there was a giant ticking clock hanging over everything. The soldiers knew the war was winding down, and they wanted to get their victory before they ran out of time.

But all I had was time. While I waited, I read the books I brought, wrote e-mails home, and went to the gym. But going to the gym had to be timed just right. You didn't want to do it early in the morning or late at night because at both those times the crowds hit. Lunch was also bad.

I tried to go after breakfast. I also tried to go when there weren't a lot of SEALs in the gym. These guys are exactly like they're advertised to be. Unlike the Green Berets, who for the most part look like linebackers, SEALs look like models. Their muscles are cut and chiseled and they all seem to care about what they look like. And I say that as a compliment. Being a Virginia Beach kid, I have a healthy respect for the Navy's special operators. I've spent many a night trying to stay on the good side of a gang of SEALs at Hot Tuna, a local Virginia Beach bar.

Unlike what I had seen on past trips, now the Navy had invaded the Green Berets' southern Afghanistan home. Months before their most famous raid, and that was an even more elite group of SEALs, the Navy's "swimming Rangers" had appropriated their own section of the camp. And while there was a fragile peace in place, the two special operations tribes were always on the verge of a blowup. They might all be on the same team, but like a good family, there was lots of infighting.

And the SEALs and Green Berets fought like brothers over the last cinnamon roll.

Let's first explain that Special Forces see the war in Afghanistan as their war. They were the first in, after the CIA. They were the ones who rode horses and chased the Taliban out of Afghanistan. They'd also captured Kandahar, and set up Camp Brown. So, the SEALs were houseguests.

Too often Special Forces are confused with special operations units like the SEALs, Rangers, Pararescue, combat controllers, Psy Op, and Civil Affairs. All of them are special operations, but only the Green Berets are Special Forces. The Marines have their own command, which was created in 2006, but they are still sorting out their exact role. They modeled themselves after the Green Berets and merged their adviser units with Force Recon, but lacked the history and experience that came with the green beret and were still muddling through what it meant to be part of the community.

The Special Forces motto, *de oppresso liber*, Latin for "to free the oppressed," reflects the units' historical mission of training guerrillas against an occupying power. The teams are based, in part, on the Jedburgh teams from World War II that were sent to France and other occupied nations to work with resistance units.

Formed in 1952, 10th Special Forces Group was the first of the units created to operate behind enemy lines after a Soviet invasion of Western Europe to be deployed. Based in Bad Tölz, Germany, the rest of the cadre soon formed more Special Forces units to help train soldiers in Vietnam, where Moore wrote the Green Berets book.

Most of the other units are trained to break things (Rangers and SEALs) or other specialty missions dealing with influencing the enemy or population or managing relief efforts and projects. The Air Force brought some special skills to the mix, with a focus on linking aircraft to the mission (calling in air strikes or air traffic control) or as medics.

Going into the gym, I saw the best example of the interservice fighting that makes living and working around the different tribes fun.

Posted on the door of the gym, and in several other places around the camp, was a flyer. It had a picture of a bunch of SEALs, without shirts, posing on a pier. A SEAL trident badge sat on the top center.

THE TRIDENT WORKOUT

1. REMOVE SHIRT
2. TURN ON POP MUSIC
3. THROW NECK PAD
4. YELL AND SCREAM
5. DROP WEIGHTS ON THE FLOOR
6. BREAK EQUIPMENT (DO NOT ATTEMPT TO REPAIR)
7. FOLLOW GIRLS AROUND THE GYM (THEY LIKE IT!!!)
8. ADJUST BANDANNA
9. STARE IN MIRROR (10 MINS IS ACCEPTABLE)
10. REPEAT

THE ONLY EASY DAY . . . WAS YESTERDAY!!!

By lunch, most of the flyers were gone, torn down by SEALs or others who didn't want to see things get out of hand. I found out from some Green Berets that the "workout" was written by an Army sergeant tired of what he perceived as the SEALs lack of respect for the camp. That kind of grumbling was constant. I'd been to Camp Brown with other Special Forces Groups, who always complained about the previous unit's camp maintenance.

But the daggers came out when it was SEALs because while the Special Forces liked to call themselves "Quiet Professionals," they really craved some of the attention paid to their Navy cousins. Hell, who doesn't? Would you risk your life for no glory? I know it was unpopular to admit it, but some glory or at least respect was part of the payoff. So, like the Marines, who have convinced a nation that the whole force is elite, the SEALs had the special operations publicity machine on lockdown.

They also had their own workout. The next day, the SEALs responded on the white board at the gym:

ODA GYM RULES

1. CONCEAL MUFFIN TOP W/ T-SHIRT
2. ROCK OUT TO COLD PLAY
3. DISCUSS FID—FAIL [FID is foreign internal defense or training foreign troops]
4. USE NECK PAD
5. COMMENCE JANE FONDA WORKOUT
6. BE GENTLE
7. FOLLOW EACH OTHER AROUND GYM—THAT'S GAY
8. ADJUST BERET
9. STARE AT THE SEALs (NO CARBS SINCE 2004!!!)
10. ERASE BEFORE GIRLS SEE

To the Green Berets' credit, the notice stayed on the board for the whole day. No doubt they did this as a way to give themselves motivation to plot a proper response. But I wasn't around to see the next salvo. My plan to go out to a village had been changed. Now I was going to be with a team training the Afghan National Civil Order Police.

An FID mission, and one that merged with the strategy to train the Afghans so that they can fight for themselves. But what does a soldier know about being a cop? Not much, until you realize that the criminals they're chasing are insurgents armed with bombs and machine guns.

CHAPTER 3

ODA 7316

After almost a week of travel and logistics, I'd finally made it to my first team.

I climbed into a beat-up van with Jeremy and Ben, and we made the fifteen-minute ride from the main base to Camp Simmons, a satellite post on the outskirts of Kandahar Airfield. As we drove toward Simmons, I saw aircraft ranging from fighters to massive military and civilian cargo planes bringing in supplies and men. With the surge in full swing, hundreds of new soldiers and tons of supplies and equipment were arriving at the base daily.

The airfield was the center of the Coalition universe in southern Afghanistan. Mushrooming over the years into a small city that hugs the southern side of the runway, it was home to more than thirty thousand Coalition soldiers, American service members, and contractors. The roar of jets taking off and landing created the base's twenty-four-hour sound track, and military trucks and civilian 4x4 Toyotas, Land Cruisers, and other SUVs in all shapes and sizes clogged the roads. Base police patrolled the roads and gave out tickets and there was even an open-air market where soldiers could buy food, trinkets, and get coffee at Tim Hortons or a burger at T.G.I. Friday's.

Kandahar Army Airfield was not Afghanistan. It was a weird Western enclave that grew up around an airstrip. Simmons wasn't much better. Next to the main Afghan Army camp, the base was used by the Special Forces team that was partnered with the commandos.

The Afghans' elite force, the commandos, were trained and mentored by Special Forces to undertake raids. On one of the sexier missions, a team spent their whole rotation training commandos, helicoptering into hot spots, and spending no more than forty-eight hours hunting and killing the enemy before coming back.

But I wasn't going to embed with a team doing that mission. My team was partnered with the Afghan National Civil Order Police (ANCOP). They were teaching the country's top cops to patrol and set checkpoints in Kandahar.

The team—ODA 7316—was from the 7th Special Forces Group based at Fort Bragg. They were experts in Latin America. But since there was a high demand for Special Forces soldiers in Afghanistan, they often took a rotation in central Asia.

And since the battalion in charge of southern Afghanistan was from the 3rd Special Forces Group, the 7th Group teams didn't get the top missions. There was a lot of talk about everyone being on the same team, but the Special Forces soldiers, like the SEALs, shun other services, and the rivalry stretches to the different groups. I've seen two teams at the same firebase fight over a training area.

So, while the ANCOP mission was necessary, it wasn't sexy. But it was a good example of what the Green Berets do well: train native troops. And I didn't want to sit around the headquarters any longer. My original embed was off the table.

Less than twelve hours before I was supposed to join a convoy to the village, Ben and Jeremy came to my door. When I opened it, I knew. They had that exasperated look that only comes from fighting the good fight with the chain of command and losing.

"I wouldn't worry about packing up," Crisp said. "And we need to get you out of here. There are VIPs coming."

My stuff was half packed and lying on the adjacent bed. As I piled it into the backpack, Jeremy told me how the generals in Kabul put an embargo on embeds to teams doing village stability. So my only choice was to see how they trained Afghan cops.

"The ANCOP guys are over at Simmons," Crisp said. "I talked to the captain and they have a mission tomorrow. I'll take you and Ben over tomorrow after lunch."

Simmons was nothing to brag about. Built on the same gravel and moon dust that covers most of southern Afghanistan, it was a cluster of drab, tan huts with a two-story barracks for the teams living at the camp. The camp butted up against a bigger base where a hodge-podge of soldiers and contractors worked and was part of the main Afghan Army base in the province. The camps were separated by a gate, and the Green Berets at Simmons would go to the bigger American camp to eat and play volleyball.

I'd been there the year before and knew the layout. But it was more crowded than I remembered. Obama's surge included more than just conventional forces. There were more teams in country and two were backed into Simmons.

Arriving at the camp, Ben and I were greeted by Courtney, the captain in charge of the team. He met us in front of his operations center, a small office room with a wooden desk built along its perimeter. One part office, one part storage area, and one part clubhouse, it was the center of activity for the team on Simmons.

Courtney was lean with dark skin and a chiseled frame. Prone to doing pull-ups near the chow hall before every meal, he moved like an athlete, but spoke in a very calm, low voice. We shook hands and he walked us toward the operations center.

"I've got to finish these slides," he said. "You guys can wait in here. We'll do the premission brief in about a half hour."

Courtney had a confident air about him, but not cocky. He was a former company commander from the 10th Mountain Division, and this was his second deployment to Afghanistan. His first tour, in 2006, had been in the eastern part of the country. This was his first tour as an ODA commander.

Ushering us through the door, the captain told us to wait while he finished up some last-minute details for the mission. On his screen was a detailed plan showing checkpoints set up by the ANCOP a day earlier in Kandahar City. The team was going to spend the afternoon checking on the police and plotting GPS fixes on the checkpoints in the event they came under attack. The team could then race to the police officers' aid.

It was a simple mission and one that they'd agreed to let me ride along on. I hoped it would be the start of a steady diet of missions, but first I had to pass the sniff test. I've never met a team that wanted to have a reporter tag along. We don't bring a lot to the fight. I'm not sure how my pen, a camera, or a notebook is going to do much when the shooting starts. That is one of the reasons I try to be seen and not heard during missions.

While I could not participate as a team member, I did have a role. On the ground, I knew that my best bet to survive was to be as little trouble as possible and to make friends as fast as possible. And the best way into a team or unit was through the top noncommissioned officer. In this case, it was Tony, the team's sergeant.

Shaking my hand, Tony told me to make myself at home. Like the rest of the team, he kept me at arm's length. I'd been forced upon them, I was sure, and they were just focused on getting through the day.

Tony sat next to Courtney. The team's top enlisted leader, Tony was a sergeant first class and was taking over as team sergeant for the first time. Short with a barrel chest and a black mustache and shaggy hair, he spoke softly and, despite not engaging in small talk, had an almost friendly air about him.

After a quick hello, he turned back to his computer. Grabbing a foldout chair, I waited until I was spoken to. I noticed that Tony was wearing a team T-shirt. The team had taken the "Gentleman Bastards" as its nickname. The team logo, for this deployment, was a devil. He had long red horns, a thin mustache and thick goatee, and was smoking a massive cigar.

On the back, there was a Cormac McCarthy quote from *Blood Meridian or the Evening Redness in the West:* "War was always here. Before man was, war waited for him. The ultimate trade awaiting its ultimate practitioner."

A heady quote and the first time I'd seen a McCarthy quote on a team shirt.

Since we had a few minutes to kill, I sat quietly and watched Tron, the team's Mexican-American intelligence sergeant, work on a computer with three monitors. He was going over satellite images of the team's new base outside of Kandahar. The team was scheduled to take their ANCOP out to the Zhari district in a couple of weeks.

They were scheduled to leave Kandahar after the holiday known as Eid, a Muslim celebration at the end of Ramadan, the holy month of fasting, and set up a firebase in the Zhari district. The ANCOP were going to set up checkpoints along Highway One in hopes of stemming the flow of guns and fighters in and out of Kandahar. Both the Coalition and the Taliban knew that the next big battle in the war would go down in the city and both sides were "prepping" the battlefield.

Taped to the walls were maps of the surrounding area. The countryside around Kandahar was a safe haven for Taliban fighters. Since the movement was born in the districts around Afghanistan's second largest city, the Taliban operated freely in many of the villages.

The importance of Kandahar could not be downplayed. It was the capital of Afghanistan under Taliban rule and is the heart of the Pashtun tribes, which make up the majority of Taliban fighters and supporters.

Stuck on the map were several pushpins, each one showing the location of a checkpoint on the highway. The road was the main avenue in and out of the western part of the city and one of the most heavily bombed tracks in the country.

I only sat there for a few minutes, but it felt like much longer. Waiting sucks in general, but it was much worse when you were also trying to find a way to build rapport. The few times I tried to talk with Ben, it felt awkward. Since Courtney, Tony, and Tron were all working, our voices sounded loud. At one point, Ben got up to smoke a cigarette. At that moment I wished I smoked too since it would free me from having to wait quietly.

Soon, other members of the team crowded into the ops center. All were fit, with tattoos peeking out of their sleeves. Gregg, the team's senior medic, came in first to find his weapon on the floor. Snatching it up, he wiped the dust from the barrel.

"Who did this to you, baby?" he whispered to his M4 rifle, giving his teammates an accusatory look.

I had watched as the Air Force J-TAC, John, knocked it over when he was getting a bottle of water from a small dorm-room-size refrigerator in the corner. While the bulk of a Special Forces team is made up of soldiers, the team often has support guys—including airmen—with very specialized skills, like John, who had the ability to call in air strikes.

"Sorry, man," John said through a thick black beard. "Must have fell when I got a water."

"Shitbag," Gregg said jokingly as he continued to clean off his weapon.

Body armor, weapons, and helmets covered the open space in the room. All of these items went into what was called a "kit," and each team member set up his body armor with pouches for gear according to his preferences.

With his weapon clean, Gregg came over to me. "I'm Gregg," he said, shaking my hand. "You have a first-aid kit?"

Each soldier had an Individual First-Aid Kit (IFAK) on his body armor. As the senior medic, Gregg was in charge of keeping everybody healthy, even writers who were tagging along. I didn't have one, which earned me a disapproving look.

"Get with me when we get back," he said. "I'll get you an IFAK."

The room at this point was crowded with the team and their attachments. Standing next to the captain was the team's law enforcement liaison, Mike the Cop, who was a sheriff in Wilmington, North Carolina. Nearby by was Bowman, a mechanic from Mississippi, who spoke with a syrupy southern accent and had a thin mustache that looked like a dirt stain. The team mocked his accent, but knew that he was the reason why the trucks they needed to patrol ran.

"He makes sure the trucks have oil," Gregg said, but pronounced the word *oil* in an almost grunt with a long *O*.

The team laughed.

Clean-cut with a look that mirrored a model in a men's magazine, Gregg was the team's mouth, quick with a comment about almost everybody and everything. Nothing was said or done without Gregg voicing his opinion about it, sometimes to the chagrin of Courtney and Tony.

But today, Gregg's commentary earned only laughs. When Tron started to give the intelligence report, Gregg was quick to mock his accent, which was halting, with bits of English coming out in a mumble. The words started and stopped like the man who was speaking them was having a seizure.

"Can we get a translator?" Gregg said.

Unlike in other units, a sense of humor is often welcome in Special Forces units.

The premission briefing covers the purpose of the mission, where we were going (center of Kandahar City), and who was riding where. It was the end of Ramadan and the city spent the night celebrating Eid. With the fasting over now, the team was ready for an increase in attacks. One of the biggest threats besides IEDs were suicide bombers. A few days before, the Taliban stole two Afghan police trucks.

"If you see any vehicles or motorcycles coming at the convoy, do what you have to do, but do it smartly," Courtney said.

I was in the second truck with Mike the Cop; the team's dog handler, Jake, and his working dog, Apollo; and Matt, the team's senior weapons sergeant. When I got to the truck, Matt was wearing a black Deception baseball cap backward. Around his waist was a belt holding a dozen 40mm grenades.

With an almost Joker-like grin plastered across his face, Matt welcomed me aboard the massive MRAP—Mine Resistant Ambush Protected—armored truck. After showing me where to sit, he went about setting up his station. First, he took out a long, black can of Monster energy drink. Then he strapped his backpack, with his rifle in a pouch on the back, to the truck. Finally, he fished out his headphones for the radio.

The trucks were massive armored behemoths that looked like something out of a postapocalyptic road movie. There was a main gun on the top controlled by the gunner in the main cabin and another machine gun on the rear of the truck. That one required one of the team—Jake, on this trip—to stand exposed behind it.

Matt was on the main gun, but he'd have preferred to be outside in a turret rather than behind a monitor inside the truck.

"It is better situational awareness. I can hear things. I can see around me," he said as he settled in behind the monitor.

The twelve-inch monitor offered a limited view of the area around the truck despite its ability to switch to infrared and its night-vision capabilities. The joystick that moved the .50-caliber machine gun resembled a fighter pilot's stick with a flip-up red safety and a trigger. Matt could rotate the gun almost 360 degrees, zooming in to a target and switching to different sensors.

As we motored toward the gate, we talked about past deployments. Since I'd been to Gardez, where Matt had been stationed last deployment, we quickly started to tell war stories. I started with a story about going through the Khost-Gardez Pass. The road—at least what they call a road in Afghanistan—weaves up over the mountains between the two provinces along Afghanistan's eastern border.

It's more cliff than road, and when I was on it, there were no guardrails. At points, the road was just wide enough to let two trucks pass. Without the guardrails, you were either hugging the rock face or trying to keep your tires on the edge of the road, with a view of nothing but sky above and the valley floor below.

Matt had been on the same road on his last deployment. He was in a truck much like the one we were riding in today and said that having to focus on the monitor while the truck swayed had given him motion sickness. He got about halfway to his destination when the nausea kicked in.

"I could see rocks or sky in the monitor," Matt said. "I grabbed a garbage bag, and by the end of the trip, I was puking up stuff I didn't remember eating. I was combat-ineffective for sure."

Settling into the seat right behind the driver—but facing Matt, who was seated behind the gun console—I pulled out a bag of sunflower seeds. This patrol involved mostly driving, which was boring. And I had a bad habit of falling asleep in cars. So, the jolt of salt and the effort of breaking the shells and spitting the seeds kept me alert.

The same seemed to be true for Matt, who called the seeds "Mormon dip." Matt was by far the most enthusiastic and personable guy on the team, and we were barely out of the gate when we were well into our third of fourth topic of conversation: Matt's only bad habits.

"Monster drinks and tattoos," he says in an almost manic tone, taking a sip of a massive, twenty-four-ounce Monster energy drink. "I don't drink or smoke."

Matt was lanky and tall with long lean muscles and thick veins that crisscrossed his arms underneath the many tattoos that covered most of his arms.

"I can clear out a pool party when I take off my shirt," he joked about his tattoos.

The Mormon Church looks askance at tattoos, but Matt had at least half a dozen, including ANGELS AND DEMONS tattooed on his right arm. That tattoo and the Deception hat were at the core of Matt's personality. He struggled to reconcile his two worlds. He never mixed his team friends with his Mormon friends, and he often said that he was two different people depending on the company he was with.

"I try to be religious and follow the rules of the LDS people, but at the same time I am out dealing death," is how he put it.

Matt was one of the more senior members of the team. He had

been in the unit for more than two years. Matt grew up outside of Salt Lake City. He'd been an adventurer all his life, working in Alaska as a nature guide for a while before going to school at Utah Valley University. He was studying to be a nurse, but got bored and joined the Army instead. This was his last adventure before he planned to return to Utah and settle into the typical Mormon lifestyle.

"Lots of kids," he joked.

At the recruiters' officer, he saw the poster of an infantryman and told them that that was what he wanted to do. He enlisted under a now-defunct program that allowed someone to serve only eighteen months, not including basic training. At the time the war in Iraq was raging and the Army was having trouble finding recruits. It was a good way to allow people to volunteer, get their war on, and get out without making too big of a commitment.

About halfway through basic training, his drill instructor pulled him aside and told him about the eighteen-month X-Ray program, a Special Forces recruiting pipeline that allowed people to join Special Forces off the street. Liking what he heard, Matt transferred into the X-Ray program, got selected, and started training. At first, he wanted to be a medical sergeant, but quickly switched weapons. He didn't have a lot of guns as a kid, but always had an interest in them.

"People are made for certain things and I was made to be a soldier," he said as we rumbled toward Kandahar City. "It isn't work for me. It's fun."

During the X-Ray training, he tested out of Spanish and Portuguese, which he'd learned on his Mormon mission. He spent a year in São Paolo, Brazil. His religious mission served as a good base for his future Special Forces career. Both are about going to a foreign land, building rapport, and spreading either the word of God or the tenets of democracy, depending on the mission.

"It is all hearts and minds, but in one you hand out books instead of bullets," he said.

This was his second deployment to Afghanistan. He had also deployed to Colombia and Brazil for jungle school in April 2009. He did this for two reasons: one, he wanted to be one of the select few foreigners who was able to complete the school, and two, he wanted to be able to tell the stories. Matt was only the twenty-second American ever to complete the grueling jungle school training, which teaches survival skills and tactics . . . if you can survive the school.

The instructors were borderline sadistic and sleep deprivation played an inordinately large role in the curriculum. Exhausted students have been known to shoot themselves by accident; others have died as a result of falling out of a tree and landing on their machetes. One student in the class before Matt's got "caught by the river monster," as Matt put it.

The students had to swim twelve kilometers in full gear at night.

"Swim to the light," the instructors yelled at Matt and his fifteen-man team.

As they waded in, he could feel his fatigues get heavy. The soldiers who didn't waterproof their rucksacks watched as the packs sank like anchors. Soon Matt was swimming far from shore. A few soldiers started to drown. Instructors in a boat nearby just tossed them life jackets. Occasionally they would shine a spotlight at the shore. Matt could see the glowing eyes of alligators in the jungle. Just as they got close to the light, which was on the back of another boat, the boat's motor started and it rumbled farther away.

"I just smiled and kept swimming," he said. "If I am not sucking, I am not having a good time. What is that line from *A League of Their Own*? 'It is the hard that makes it great.'"

To celebrate his graduation from the school, he got the number "22" tattooed on his left arm with a panther's head, the symbol of the jungle school. That was the only boasting you'd ever hear from Matt.

Gregg told me later that Matt was the quintessential Green Beret.

"Among the most quietly deadly individuals I've been around," he said of him. "He's just so competent. He never stops thinking."

Just outside the gate, the team met the ten police officers who would show them the checkpoints on the road between their camp and Kandahar Airfield. It was my first glimpse of the ANCOP, who dressed in the same green uniform as their National Police cousins.

Following the ANCOP's Humvees, we started toward the city. Between the airfield and the city, there were a few compounds and some scrubby fields. But once we got through a small pass between two small mountains to the west of the airfield, we could see the outskirts of Kandahar City.

The biscuit-colored city with its flat adobe-like buildings and monotonous color looked like a location in a *Star Wars* movie. A thin dusty haze hung over the city as the team drove into its outskirts. The closer we got to the city center, the thicker the traffic became. There were no traffic laws and cars weaved in and out, searching for the path of least resistance.

Speeding cars shared the road with men on bikes or motorcycles. The team kept a keen eye on each one, on the lookout for the lone biker who was known to shoot out of the many alleyways with a bomb strapped to his gas tank.

But to those of us who were sitting up in the armored truck, the town felt distant. To me, it was almost like I was watching the unfolding streets on a screen. The thick armor blocked out all the noise and smells. There was no dust and the thick glass distorted the view, making things seem out of whack. It was like watching Kandahar pass through a hall of mirrors. Everything Matt had said about not knowing his surroundings and fighting like a robot through a monitor now made sense to me. It was impossible to get any real sense of the city.

For the next three hours, we drove to each checkpoint. At each one, the captain marked the GPS coordinates and we moved to the next one. Except for some traffic, the mission was uneventful.

Boring really.

But it had offered me my first glimpse of this team. Afterward, we made plans to meet the following afternoon for shooting practice. There was a nearby range and the men wanted to zero their sniper rifles.

The invitation was welcomed and probably meant that I'd passed the first sniff test at least.

CHAPTER 4

ROCKET ATTACK

Regardless of their specialties, all Green Berets like to shoot.

Medics. Engineers. Communications sergeants. A Green Beret who can't shoot is an impossibility. And even the worst shot in the regiment is still better than most soldiers. But among men who never admitted defeat or inferiority, you didn't want to be the worst shot. Like everything else in this world, shooting was just another way to measure dick size.

Going out to the range was the closest thing to playtime the team ever got to experience, so when they asked me and Ben to take part, we accepted. Manny, the team's senior communications sergeant, and Matt set up the sniper rifles first. They zeroed the scopes and took turns pinging the metal silhouette two hundred meters away. Manny, finished with his weapon, called me over and let me take the final shots.

Crawling behind the scope, I could hear Matt and Gregg line up another shot. The shot was a muffled crack as the suppressor stifled the boom and I heard Matt say "good shot" to Gregg.

Manny helped me get comfortable behind the gun and talked me through the process of aiming and firing. When I stared into the scope, the target was suddenly huge. Moving the crosshairs around, I finally settled on what I hoped was the target's chest. The trigger was smooth and my first shot hit with a loud *ping*.

"Slow your trigger pull," Manny said as I lined up another shot.

The second *ping* came easier. It hit the target again and I popped up. Shit, if I missed every target from this point on, I'd still be happy. Manny complimented my shooting as he picked up the gun and put it back into the truck. I had pretty low expectations, and hitting the target kept my cool points intact.

Manny didn't have Matt's energy or Gregg's mouth. He brought a calm to everything and at thirty-five was one of the old men on the team. At a glance, Manny, with his long scraggly beard and dark eyes, looked Afghan or Asian. But he was born in Texas and grew up all over the American West. His parents were Vietnam vets who eventually split, leaving him and his brothers. He'd eventually hook up with his birth father as a teenager, but things didn't go well. Manny was eventually shipped to a boys' ranch in Utah.

"I got into a lot of fights when I was a kid," he told me later.

He eventually moved to Montana and lived with his grandparents. He completed most of high school there, but moved back to Texas to be with his father his senior year. He signed up for the Army in Texas, part of an early enlistment program, but never went.

Instead, he, like Matt, took a mission to Brazil for the Mormon Church. He spent two years in the 1990s working in rural Brazil and living in almost poverty conditions. He lived on about ninety dollars a month and worked tirelessly for the church. He was happy, he said, if where he lived was somewhat dry and he had some food. He was nineteen when he went and was used to being on his own. The mission, like Matt's, helped him gain skills he'd eventually use in the Special Forces.

I noticed after the first day that Manny had a quiet confidence to him. He never got excited or too angry. After learning about his upbringing, I got a sense that he had seen tough times and there was little out there that he couldn't overcome.

After his Mormon mission, he moved to Provo, Utah, and started selling pest control door-to-door with his brother. He still wanted to be in the military and joined the Utah National Guard's 19th Special Forces Group in 1996.

Just after joining, he met his wife at a dance. Two weeks after their first date, they were engaged. But Manny was already committed to the Army, so he left soon after to go to training. He completed basic training, advanced training, and airborne school.

Selection was hard because he didn't have a lot of experience in ruck marching. He was a new private and lacked the knowledge of senior sergeants who'd been in the service for years. But Manny kept his head down and kept marching, despite stress fractures he suffered in his feet.

"I reminded myself just to take it a day at a time," he said. "You just have to believe in yourself. To me, it is all mental. You don't have to be the fastest or the strongest. Guys that talk a lot don't make it. It is amazing how a lot of guys will talk themselves out of it. You have to have self-confidence."

Back at 19th Group, he worked odd jobs in construction and at a treadmill factory between deployments to Korea, Thailand, and as many schools as he could take. And he quickly had three kids, including twins, in less than three years of marriage.

After 9/11, his team was activated. They went from Utah to Fort Campbell, in Kentucky, and eventually to Afghanistan. They arrived near Khost in April 2002 and took control of 250 Afghan fighters. They lived in caves and patrolled near the border. Most of their hits were dry holes, and the most exciting thing to happen to them was a flood that wiped out their trucks.

Weeks after he got back to the States, Manny requested a transfer to active duty and was assigned to 7th Group in January 2003. He deployed with Matt and Mike, the team's senior engineer, to Afghanistan in 2008 and to Colombia.

With the most time on the team, he acted as the group's moral compass. He was the one the others went to for advice or to bitch. He not only had the military experience, but the life skills that were needed to cope with the day-to-day stress and the interpersonal dynamics of the team.

"I have the ability to see where people are coming from," Manny told me. "I try to eliminate the drama. It is just wasteful."

So far, the shoot had been drama-free.

Moving down to the other targets, we spent the next two hours shooting M4 rifles and pistols at targets with several circles. Since Matt was running the range, he allowed me to shoot his M203, which has a grenade launcher attached underneath the barrel. It is heavier than the M4, and Matt had a different sight on his rifle, which had more magnifying power than the others, which came in handy later. The team practiced switching from rifle to pistol. They can do this smoothly and keep their shots grouped tightly together.

Gregg took the targets to my left. Between magazines, he offered pointers or at least a constant commentary on how well he was shooting. Gregg named his weapons. His M4, with a short barrel, was called "the Foe Hammer" (written on a small tape on the butt stock), and his Glock pistol was "Heartbreaker," because of its close range.

"They are my babies. They are the things that are going to save me," he said.

But with all the warrior bravado, there was also a true love of medicine. Being the medic was something Gregg took seriously. Not only did he want to be the best gun in a fight, so the team would win, but he also understood that his men counted on him to keep them alive. It was a responsibility that he readily accepted, but knew that if he ever began to doubt his ability, he'd leave the team.

"If I didn't think I could handle someone getting shot, I'd move to the B-team," he told me.

But right now all he wanted to do was shoot. And talk.

After a while Matt pulled out a series of zombie targets. One zombie was dressed up like a gang member and the other was a Nazi SS officer. I have a special hatred for the Nazis, mostly because I watched too many Indiana Jones movies, and relished shooting the targets full of holes. Again, while Gregg bragged nearby about hitting the zombie's brain, the only way to kill a zombie of course, it was an achievement even with the help of a laser sight for me to hit the target at all.

The last exercise was a stress shoot. Going back to the hundred-meter berm, you fired ten shots. Then you moved up to seventy-five meters and fired ten more. Fifty meters, ten more. Then you changed magazines and fired ten more walking toward the target, for a total of forty shots. Taped to our target was a water bottle. The idea was to hit the bottle on your first shot, preferably. If not that, to at least hit it. During this part of the practice, the team was not allowed to use their magnifying sights, which made it harder to hit the target and so was a better test of their skills.

Courtney went first.

As Matt yelled and sprayed water on him, the captain fired and moved closer and closer to the water bottle. Manny, tucked behind a sniper scope, called off the action like a play-by-play announcer. After the first ten shots, Manny offered an update.

"The water bottle is still holding strong," he said.

Being the only officer on the team meant that the other guys watched closely to see how he did. Trotting back to the line, the captain came out with a respectable twenty-two out of forty shots and broke the water bottle.

"I'll tell you what, if that was PowerPoint, he would have killed it," Gregg said.

A common joke in the Army. Sergeants work for a living. Officers push paper and sit behind computers. When the captain wasn't training or meeting with locals, he was often stuck at his desk creating briefing slides. He didn't like it, no officer did, but it was part of his job. The comment earned a chuckle, and soon everyone was focusing on the next shooter. For the most part, the team members ranked about the same. Some, like Matt and Gregg, did better than others.

Toward the end, Matt told me it was my turn.

I used Matt's M203 again. Sliding behind the berm, I started to focus on the target. The water bottle looked small even in the sight. I could hear Matt's boots crunching the dirt and rocks nearby, so I just aimed at the center and hoped for the best. Then I saw Matt's shadow cover me as he bent down and flipped a switch on the scope. Soon the target looked like it was within arm's reach.

Matt yelled, "Go!" and I started shooting.

Before long, I was racing toward the target. Slamming myself to the ground, I fired another round of shots. Panting and bleeding from a gash in my knee, I kept going. More concerned with going full speed and not embarrassing myself, I didn't really focus on anything other than what I saw through the sight. Nearby, small flash-bang grenades exploded. A few times, Matt fired his 9mm pistol at the berm while I lined up the shots. While I switched magazines, Matt reached down and switched the magnification back so that I could see as I walked toward the target firing.

As the last round ripped through the target, I was smoked and could barely keep the rifle steady. Putting the rifle on safe, I stood and watched Matt count the holes.

"Thirty-five, thirty-six, thirty-seven, thirty-eight . . ."

And no water bottle.

He counted twice. On paper, I was a sharpshooter. In reality, I'd had an unfair advantage. I had the laser sight on 4x instead of 1x, so the target was close. The others had actually had to shoot with some skill.

But I still left the range with my dignity, except for torn pants. When I dove to the ground to set up behind a berm, I tore them open and cut my knee. A trickle of blood was running down my leg. Clinging to the back of one of the pickup trucks, I noticed that I'd also torn the crotch out of the pants.

As we headed back to the camp, Gregg and Josh, the team's other communications sergeant, asked me and Ben if we wanted to go with them to dinner at TGIF.

And yes, I am talking about the chain restaurant.

Ben and I met Josh, Gregg, Jake, the dog handler, and John at T.G.I. Friday's about an hour later.

Most of us had simply changed into shorts and clean T-shirts, but Gregg showed up like he was back home and going out on a date. Tight T-shirt over his sculpted chest and thick arms, dark designer jeans, cuffed perfectly at the ankle, and flip-flops. It looked like he'd stepped out of a men's-magazine fashion spread.

The team joked that Gregg was the prettiest of the bunch. And he'd tell you the team was right. His hair was cut precisely, and his sideburns were well-groomed. Gregg owned a variety of rescue service or team T-shirts, which he wore with either a Yankees or Detroit Tigers cap (the latter was a gift from a good friend; Gregg himself was a Yankee fan).

Settling into a table near the window, the guys and Ben set about ordering a feast. Potato skins, wings, burgers. Ben started a milkshake trend, and the rest ordered one too and sucked them down with smiles.

The dinner conversation bounced from football and baseball to the absurdity of having a T.G.I. Friday's in Afghanistan.

TGIF was part of the "boardwalk," a collection of stores and restaurants on Kandahar Airfield. It was the center of the social scene and one of the few places where soldiers from all nations mingled. There was a French, German, Canadian, and Dutch PX—think Target or Walmart. The American PX was about a block away and actually looked like a small-town Walmart. Two coffee shops. A pizza place. A Subway. A KFC and stores selling Afghan rugs and other artifacts.

Everything was built around a wooden walkway. It was like something out of the Wild West. Everybody had a gun either over their shoulder or dangling from a holster. At night, it was jammed with soldiers blowing off steam. At the center of the boardwalk were volleyball nets and a hockey rink, brought in by the Canadians, with boards, metal hockey nets, and even benches with doors for storing things under.

Going to the boardwalk passed for a nightly ritual for the soldiers who lived on the base and certainly for those who passed through. There wasn't that much to do when you weren't working and it was about the only place where you could people-watch. Think of it like the town square.

For the Special Forces soldiers, it was a perfect place to observe and comment upon those who did everything but fight the war. The collection of soldiers, contractors, and airman eating nearby were a motley group. Many of them looked pretty physically unfit as they stuffed burgers into their mouths.

"We were over at the kebab place the other day and I saw this airman come up," Gregg says. "In the magazine well of his M16, he has a pack of cigarettes."

Seeing the cigarettes in the magazine well set him off.

"At least try and act like you're in the military," Gregg said. "There's tons of foreign military dudes walking around. It's a god-damn disgrace."

Gregg and Matt later saw a Navy officer with her disassembled pistol wrapped in three plastic bags. Gregg thought Matt was going to have a fucking heart attack.

As far as the team was concerned, a weapon was a precision tool, and had to be treated as such. It was the only thing that stood in the way of living or dying on the battlefield. And not just for them. For their buddy too. But on Kandahar Airfield, a weapon was something a soldier had to lug around as he or she went shopping or to get coffee. Almost all of the rifles and pistols were dusty, the sights were likely off from being banged around, and the female soldiers often carried their rifles like a purse.

Josh laughed.

"Hey man, it's pretty cool if you can carry your cigarettes that way," he said in a mocking, nasal voice.

The contempt on the faces of the team members was obvious. It irked Gregg to think that there were soldiers and airmen who would spend a year on Kandahar Airfield, work in air-conditioned offices, go to the boardwalk, and fly back on a plane. That would be "their" war.

But like everybody else in the restaurant, the objects of the team's contempt were just seeking a little normalcy. A reprieve from life in Afghanistan, which was like living in biblical times but with cell phones, machine guns, and 4x4 trucks.

Unfortunately, before our potato skins arrived, the rocket attack siren sounded, yanking everyone out of the fantasy world.

A monotone voice announced the incoming rockets and a few soldiers slid off their seats and knelt under their tables. The restaurant host, a contractor from some Pacific island, lay down on the floor. A weird energy shot through the room as many of the soldiers and contractors debated whether they wanted to get down on the floor or just stay seated where they were and finish their plates of pasta primavera.

As for me, I took my cue from the team guys. I was trying to build some rapport and didn't want to mess it up by not following their lead. It was a lot like high school, with the cool kids. You tried to do what they did in order to be accepted. And so, I sat.

Josh started to joke about being killed by shrapnel from a life-size Yoda holding a light saber near the bar. All agreed that it would be embarrassing to die in a T.G.I. Friday's.

"Yeah, I can see the story about me getting killed by flying flare blasted off of the waiter's uniforms," Jake, the team's dog handler, said.

"If it hits here, I'm grabbing that banner and running," Josh said, eyeing an Alabama football banner that celebrated the school's winning of a national championship.

A native of Alabama, Josh had only a slight accent, but otherwise he was a hundred percent southern hospitality. Standing about six feet, he was not muscular like Gregg or wiry like Matt, but was just thick; if he hadn't been smiling so much of the time, he might have been intimidating.

When Josh had walked into the recruiting office in southern Alabama and joined the Army, he had one caveat. He wanted to travel. When the recruiter asked him to recite his list of dream destinations, he mentioned Panama, Germany, and Hawaii, all of which he got. Good at math, he was classed a mortarman. But after four years of carrying a mortar on foot patrols in the jungle and up mountains, Josh had had enough.

On one patrol, he was humping the mortar tube and the machine gun when he saw some MPs nearby in an air-conditioned truck.

"Big Daddy, I told myself, there is no way you're going to do this anymore," Josh told me.

He reclassed to military police so he could drive instead of walk on patrol, and eventually got deployed to Gitmo, where he guarded prisoners coming from Afghanistan.

But he soon grew bored there and went to selection. It would have been easy to judge Josh's happy-go-lucky attitude as a sign of weakness or a lack of discipline. In reality, it was just a façade, and behind it was the mind and heart of a relentlessly practical professional. Josh knew what he was good at and knew what he liked. Special Forces was the best place for him. He, like the others, knew when to get the job done.

"You don't sweat the small shit. But you better make sure your MOS"—your specialty—"is shit tight. Do your job," he told me. "We're not going to yell at you if you don't have your boots bloused."

If Gregg was the team's mouth, then Josh was its comic relief. He seemed to always have a smile peeking out of his fiery-red beard. But come mission time, he was on top of the radios, making sure the equipment worked on the trucks. It was amazing watching him run between the two keeping up a constant banter without missing any of his duties.

The more I was around Josh, the more I realized that he knew exactly what he was doing. After more than a decade in the Army, he knew his job and understood how to get it done so that once it *was* done, he could play. Poker, mostly.

He had seven years left in the Army before he got his twenty years and an Army retirement. After that, his dream job was to be a professional poker player. He was a regular on online poker sites. On his best days, he won thousands of dollars, including taking in more than thirteen thousand dollars in one tournament. He also lost, but he knew when to walk away. He had rules to playing poker. His own big-boy rules for the table.

He didn't play when he was tired.

Or when he had just fought with his wife.

Or when the kids were bombing around the house.

For Josh to be good, he needed no distractions. He needed to be locked into the game, the players, and the cards.

If poker was one of his loves, Alabama football was another. He was rarely seen without his 'Bama cap, a tan hat with a blazing crimson *A* on the front. Football was a constant topic of conversation. He could rattle off the team's schedule, mentioning how worried he was about the next stretch against Arkansas, Florida, and LSU. There are no easy weeks in the SEC and Josh knew it.

Which is why that Crimson Tide banner was going with him if the rocket hit. It didn't hit, of course, and we soon got our meals. Overall, the food was terrible. But the company was good. It was a nice change from the dining-hall rotation of Italian one day, Mexican the next, and soul food on the weekends.

After polishing off their burgers, the team members loaded up in the truck and headed back to Simmons. Since there wasn't room at their camp, I lived at Camp Brown, the special operations base on Kandahar Airfield, and would literally commute to work. But at night, some of the guys usually came over to prowl the boardwalk.

A few nights later, Josh, Gregg, Matt, John, Manny, and Bowman, the team's mechanic, returned to Kandahar Airfield to eat dinner at the All Seasons Café. Run by the Dutch, it looked like a ski lodge.

The line was almost outside of the door when Ben and I arrived.

The team was at the back waiting. Dressed in shorts, T-shirts, and 9mms, they didn't look like soldiers. More like contractors or armed teenagers.

When I walked inside I noticed a table nearby at which a group of Dutch officers was seated. They were prattling on in their native language while they devoured plates of breaded chicken cutlets and fries. Several rounds of near-beers crowded the center of the table.

Matt and Gregg were the first to order and found a table near the back. Manny was about to order when the siren for a rocket attack sounded again. This was starting to become a regular occurrence during dinner. The siren wailed and then the familiar voice boomed across the airfield.

"Rocket attack. Rocket attack."

The voice had a slight accent, which gave the alarm a "classy" touch. Not that this made any difference since, in reality, the base was so large that any rocket was likely to hit well before the alarm was sounded. Nevertheless the rockets sometimes hit close by and on occasion people were even killed. But the chances were slim.

As soon as the alarm sounded, the cashier dove to the floor like a bomb was hurtling through the window at that very moment. Nearby, the Dutch officers were on the ground covering their heads. The whole restaurant was lying on the ground waiting for the boom.

Manny, still standing holding a menu, looked perplexed. We were in a covered building. The rocket had likely already hit. He was shaking his head in disbelief, when one of the cooks peeked his head out of the kitchen and hissed at us.

"Get down. Get down."

Manny squatted and continued to look around the restaurant in disbelief. I also got on the floor and waited.

"When it is your time, it is your time," he said.

That was the mind-set of a warrior who knows that on every mission he could be facing down a machine gun. For the staff officers on the big bases, a rocket attack is a war story they can tell at home. And there, it is dangerous. But right then, it was just an obstacle to our ordering our dinners.

Soon enough, the fear subsided. The cashier, a fair-haired, fair-skinned Dutchman, got up and returned to his position and we were finally able to place our order. Back at the table, Matt was almost done with his chicken. Others also had their food and were making a big dent in the pile of fries and meat.

There was little talk since most of us were hungry. And the rocket attack left a strange energy in the place. The other diners had seen the contempt on the team's faces and didn't like the way they flaunted not getting on the ground. I could see some of the officers at the Dutch table mean-mugging us.

Then, nearby, someone dropped his rifle, and there is a collective exhale of disgust at our table.

"That is the second weapon I've seen hit the ground today," Gregg said to Matt, who just shook his head.

After dinner, we went out for milk shakes. It was Josh's idea after the tasty shakes we'd had at TGIF a few days before. But instead of entering the home of Yoda, the guys opted for a small smoothie-and-shake place on the boardwalk. Matt declined to join them and sat on the railing watching the parade of soldiers and airmen walk along the boardwalk. As each one passed, he seemed to get more and more annoyed. His body language was bristly. Across the way, the Canadians were playing street hockey in the replica rink.

Taking the shakes over to the game, we spread out on the wooden steps and watched.

The Canadians were wearing jerseys with the numbers of NHL greats like Mario Lemieux, Jaromir Jágr, and Ray Bourque. They raced around the rink thrashing a team of what looked like Americans, dressed in plain brown T-shirts and black shorts. The American team even had a female defenseman, but the Canadians attacked her like any other player. After each goal, they pumped their fists and beat on the boards with their sticks.

The game wasn't even close. The Canadians did a lot of fist pumping. It didn't look like the Americans were going to be able to pull off a miracle. With each goal, Matt seemed to get even more annoyed. After a few minutes, it looked like he'd had enough. This was a war zone. People were fighting and dying, and the Canadians were putting all their energy into a street hockey game.

"They are acting like it's game seven of the Stanley Cup," Matt said, shaking his head as the American goalie was beaten high again.

Rounding up his teammates, he and the rest returned to their base nearby. It was time to go back to their base, and hopefully soon their war.

CHAPTER 5

CORRUPTION IN DIGITAL CAMOUFLAGE

Taking care of the ANCOP was a full-time job for the team.

It seemed like every day the captain or Tony was working on some issue. The ANCOP needed food or water. Matt had an ongoing battle over some grenade launchers that the Ministry of the Interior in Kabul, the ANCOP's boss, had ordered. It seemed that the launchers wouldn't fit on the Chinese-made AK-47 rifles.

On the afternoon I met up with Tony and the captain, they were headed over to the ANCOP's compound to meet with the battalion's executive officer to talk about his concerns about the units' dearth of new digital camouflage uniforms and Roshan phone cards.

Despite the lack of roads, plumbing, and any infrastructure, Afghanistan had at least two cell-phone providers, of which Roshan was the most popular. Covering most of the populated areas of the country, it featured both English and Pashto automated customer-service messages.

The ANCOP lived in a spacious compound between Kandahar Airfield and Camp Simmons. It was brand-new and contained about a dozen barracks, a couple of large warehouses, and a massive motor pool filled with green Ford Ranger trucks and armored Humvees.

Courtney and Tony drove over to meet with the battalion's executive officer to discuss his concerns about the units' lack of new digital camouflage uniforms and Roshan phone cards.

Parking outside the barracks, Tony and Courtney, with Rza, climbed the stairs to the second floor. Rza was a former Afghan commando turned interpreter. He was one of three interpreters working with the team. The others, Big Rza and Habib, lived in a wooden building on Camp Simmons. Habib was the most vocal and social of the three. He spoke both Pashto and Dari, including the many dialects, and the money he made supported his family. Habib told his father he made seven hundred dollars a month. His father took six hundred for the family and Habib supposedly kept a hundred, but in reality he made a thousand dollars a month. This kind of "trade" was a constant of life in Afghanistan.

None of the terps tell their friends what they do for a living. Habib, who often covers his face to protect his identity, told his friends in Herāt that he was going to school in Kabul and his friends in Kabul that he was going to school in Herāt. Rza told his family, except his wife and parents, that he worked in the Afghan National Army's computer office.

Rza was lean and wiry with a dark complexion and Mongol features. Fiercely loyal to Special Forces, he berated the police officers when they didn't show gratitude to their trainers.

After I shook Rza's hand for the first time, Courtney pulled me aside.

"He has killed more people than smallpox," Courtney said.

I was told that when Rza was a commando, he was one of the best. He later went on to run the commando selection process. The story I finally got out of him was that he was on a mission when the commandos and their Special Forces mentors ran into a bunch of Taliban—called TBs by Rza—in a market. Before anyone could react, Rza was raking them with machine-gun fire. He was credited with killing most of them.

I didn't know if it was bullshit, but that was the story. And at this point, the details didn't matter because the tale had become gospel around the camp.

The white stairs leading to the second floor were filthy and a thin cloud of dust hung in the air, making everything smell musty and old. There was a faint smell of cigarette smoke as we walked down the hall and into the officers' room.

The ANCOP executive officer, Namatullah, greeted us at the door of his room. The room looked like a crackhead's hideout. It was spartanly furnished with two mattresses on the floor pushed to the wall. The mattresses had no sheets, and Namatullah and two officers sat on them while they watched a Bollywood comedy on an old color TV.

Namatullah smiled and hugged Courtney and Tony, then gestured to them to sit on the mattresses. The soldiers obliged and Namatullah squatted down on the threadbare red rug between them. Dressed in a tan G Unit T-shirt and blue Tony Soprano–style sweatpants, Namatullah looked like a middle-aged suburban dad. He even had a potbelly, and his bushy black mustache fit the cop stereotype. Resting on the rug, he folded his bare feet under him and lit a cigarette.

"Why did you not come over for Eid?" he asked Courtney. Rza

translated. Sitting behind the captain, Namatullah seemed almost bored as he stared out the window or at the TV. Despite the distractions, I got the feeling that he didn't miss a thing.

"I am busy working, trying to make sure your guys are all right," Courtney said. "Next time I will come out."

Just then a young Afghan entered the room holding three small silver platters of nuts, raisins, and candies. Pulling out a half-dozen lightly washed glass mugs, he poured us a steaming-hot round of tea. The man, who couldn't have been more than a few years past his teen years, worked for the officers and provided them with snacks and tea, served their meals, and cleaned up after them. The Afghan officers considered themselves members of a class above the common soldier, a more Soviet mentality and one that runs starkly counter to the sergeant-driven Army of the United States.

Courtney took a sip of the almost scalding liquid and placed the cup back on the floor. He knew the drill. They had to make small talk before getting to business. That morning, Courtney and the team had toured the checkpoints at the center of the city. Many of the police complained that they didn't have water or food, something Namatullah was supposed to provide.

But first they had to deal with another issue: when the commander was going to return.

The ANCOP battalion commander, Colonel Agha, had gone to Kabul for Eid. At first, he asked to leave for the holiday and Courtney told him no. His men had to work and so did he. But a day later, the battalion commander's son was in a car accident and he needed to go to Kabul on emergency leave. A fishy story, but Courtney couldn't prove that the man was lying, so he had to let him go.

"Have you heard from the commander?" Courtney asked.

"He is doing good," Namatullah said. "His son is doing good."

Right, Courtney thought. *Of course.* "When is the commander scheduled to come back?"

"He is going to call tomorrow."

Courtney shook his head.

"He can't be taking two weeks off," Courtney said. "I know you like being in command, but we need the commander back here so you can get back to you duties."

Namatullah just smiled as he picked his toes and kept one eye on the Bollywood flick as it segued into its next dance number—this one featuring courting couples prancing around the countryside, mock-boxing and generally overacting.

Courtney spent the next few minutes outlining plans for the up-coming weeks. The police would go back to patrolling in the city and training with the team after a few days off. Namatullah agreed before turning to Courtney and starting to list the problems facing his men.

No phone cards.

No new uniforms (the other battalions from Kandahar and Kabul had them).

No Eid gift.

"Nobody cares about my soldiers," Namatullah said.

He told Courtney that the team supporting his sister battalion had bought their unit phone cards and offered them gifts for Eid.

"I had a lot of missions with American Army forces in the past," Namatullah said. "They bought things for us. Has the policy changed?"

Courtney smiled. It was the only way he could hold back some of his frustration.

"All the logistics stuff is on your side of the house," Courtney said. "We don't handle that. At the end of the day, we are here to train and advise you."

Courtney knew Namatullah was trying to cajole him into giving the cops what they wanted. Too often in the past, teams had spoiled their Afghan units, showering them with equipment instead of forcing them to request it through their chain of command. Those days were long over, as more and more pressure was put on the teams to train and establish working Afghan units that could fight and sustain themselves.

"We're here to work ourselves out of a job," Courtney told me later. "It is like having a seventeen-year-old daughter living with you. She has to get a job or she will freeload off you."

But Courtney's answer wasn't what Namatullah wanted to hear. Visibly frustrated, Namatullah took his eyes off the Bollywood film, which now, for some reason, I myself couldn't stop watching. The story line seemed to have something to do with a guy with some evil twin, the two of them fighting for the same girl.

"Whenever I ask you about problems, you always tell us to talk to our chain of command. But our chain of command doesn't give a fuck about our problems," Namatullah said. "This is not like the United States."

The "fuck" was courtesy of Rza. At first, I thought that the Afghans swore as much as their American counterparts. But over time I began to strongly suspect that Rza's translations made everybody sound like a Special Forces guy. And *fuck* is not a word used sparingly in the Special Forces.

"It is impossible for us, an ODA, to feed a hundred and ninety-three guys," Courtney said. "Now there is a system in place to request supplies."

Namatullah wasn't buying it. With a look on his face like a petulant child, he listened to Courtney with his arms crossed. A frown creased his mouth.

"The money coming for ANCOP is coming from the government. They are going to cut, cut, cut, and then there is no money for ANCOP," Namatullah said. "The chain of command is stealing."

Corruption is a way of life in Afghanistan, but lately it had reached epic proportions. It had become so bad that it threatened the stability of the government the Americans and their allies were trying to prop up. As one Afghan put it: "The only way to solve the corruption problem is to round up the worst fifty culprits, put them in a plane, fly them to the United States, and crash the plane into a mountain."

"I am just worried about what will happen to my country when you guys leave," Namatullah said. "This government is going to destroy this country. The enemy of the Afghan people is the government. That is the real enemy."

The room was silent for a minute and Namatullah's words hung in the air. They had been uttered with a degree of candor that Courtney hadn't witnessed before, and he was momentarily taken aback. Namatullah's words were sobering, because in essence the team was fighting to preserve a government that some of its own people didn't want. Plus, with all the talk of withdrawal, many Afghans were concerned about what would happen to their country when the Americans left.

"At the end of the day, it starts with guys like you," Courtney said. "You need to continue to do the right thing and support your guys. Take care of your piece of the pie, as we say in the States."

The little pep talk seemed to work, as Namatullah agreed to meet with Colonel Ghulam, the ANCOP brigade commander, the next day to discuss the problems.

The next morning, Namatullah and Courtney met with Ghulam, a slim, tanned man with salt-and-pepper hair and mustache. His office was more elaborately decorated than Namatullah's room, with a wooden desk at one end and a series of couches that ran along the perimeter of the room. Rugs covered the vinyl floor.

The meeting began with some small talk about Eid, but quickly turned to uniforms and phone cards. Ghulam assured Courtney that he would check on those issues, but complained, as Namatullah had done, that he didn't have any resources.

"You need to pin on your general rank so when you make a request, you will get what you want in moments," Courtney told him.

Ghulam was supposed to be promoted to general soon, but waved off the comment.

"Rank is important in your country because you have rules," he said. "I have been in this job for one year and two days, and no one has sent me fifty cents."

It was common for Afghans to complain about resources. In all my trips to Afghanistan, I'd never heard an Afghan say he had enough or was happy with what he had.

We'd created a welfare state.

When the Americans arrived in their country, the Afghans knew that money wasn't far behind. Back at Kandahar, the stories around Camp Brown focused on some new team leader who'd been duped by some elders. The story, as I heard it, had the new team leader in a shura meeting—a meeting of the elders—finalizing plans for a project. When the team checked on the elders at the project site, they found out the elders didn't even live in the village. They were just there to collect some of the money and be on their way. Essentially, the Afghans knew how to exploit the process of obtaining projects better than the Americans did.

Namatullah sat silently during this meeting. When an Afghan soldier brought in some apples, he spent his time peeling and meticulously slicing the fruit. First he dug out the core from the top and bottom. Then, strip by strip, he slowly peeled it until it was a ball of white flesh. Finally, he cut long thin slices along the apple's width. Rarely looking up from his work, he seemed to be trying to stay clear of the debate over resources. He was content to let the captain fight his battles.

The conversation between Courtney and Ghulam went much the same as the conversation the afternoon before with Namatullah. Both sides promised to check on the uniform and phone-card requests. Ghulam assured Courtney that he would support the ANCOP.

But outside, Namatullah was defiant. He again accused Courtney of not providing for his men. He complained that the team didn't provide the police with water and food at the checkpoints.

"I don't have a golden credit card that I can go and buy food and water for all one hundred and ninety-three men," Courtney said in a stern but even voice.

Turning to me while Rza translated, he seemed a bit exasperated. It was not like he was going to change his mind and all of a sudden start buying the Afghans everything they were clamoring for. He'd made it clear during the meeting the afternoon before that the Afghans had to work through their own logistics channels.

"They are too dependent on us to get them logistics," he said to me on the ride back to Simmons.

Namatullah was upset with what the captain told him.

"I am telling you right now, if that shit happens, it is not our problem. It is your problem," Namatullah said.

He again told Courtney how the other ANCOP units were given gifts, food, and uniforms from their teams. I knew this was a lie because Courtney had talked to members of those teams the night before. They assured him that they were forcing their units to request supplies from Kabul. Courtney knew very well that all Namatullah was trying to do was play the teams against one another, manipulating them for his own ends.

"I don't want to get into this mom-and-pop stuff," Courtney said to Namatullah.

Without bending, he finally got Namatullah to put in the necessary requests to Kabul. In return, the captain promised to make a similar request through the channels on the American side in hopes of finding out what was holding up the uniforms and phone cards.

"You're like a big gun," Namatullah told Courtney. "When you hit the target, it goes boom."

Taking Courtney's hand, Namatullah invited him back to the barracks for tea. Courtney declined, instead urging Namatullah yet again to make the supply request and assuring him that he would do the same back at the American camp.

A few hours later, Courtney found out that the uniforms were in a warehouse on the ANCOP compound, and set a time to distribute them the following day.

The next day, the whole team drove to a warehouse near the ANCOP barracks and set up a line of tables. The police turned in their green uniforms in exchange for a more up-to-date digital camouflage pattern. The pattern used for the uniform looked similar to the one used by the Marine Corps.

Before the exchange began, the American team members took a set of the uniforms themselves. This was not merely a show of solidarity; it was standard practice for teams to wear the same uniform as their partner ANCOP force. This way, everyone blended in with everyone else; in the past, snipers had zeroed in on the American uniforms.

The sizes of the uniforms were a little strange and the team joked about the way they fit. Matt, who was a lean six foot three, was concerned about the pants. He figured they'd fit his slim waist, but not his long legs.

"These are my pirate pants," he joked.

While the police lined up, the team broke out sets of each size uniform for them to try on. Mike the Cop looked at the tag in one of the shirts.

"Sixty-five percent nylon and fifty percent cotton? That is some weird math," he said.

"It is a hundred and fifteen percent material," Manny said. "That just means there is fifteen percent more."

Besides the new uniform, the Afghans received new boots that were made in Kabul and resembled the American desert boot. Tony volunteered to measure their feet. The others sized the Afghans for uniform shirts, pants, and hats. Finally, they picked up a bundle of patches and Gregg, who wrote down the men's names and sizes, signed them out.

Sliding on a pair of rubber gloves, Tony started measuring for boots. The Afghans treated this procedure with some skepticism, mistrusting the measuring tool and requesting two sizes too small or too large. This led to a minor hiccup as they kept coming back to exchange their boots. The Afghans are a small people and most wear size six to nine shoes. A few wore size ten or eleven. The sizes of the boots we had went from six to eleven.

Standing among the towers of shoe boxes, I was handing each cop a pair based on Tony's measurements or the cop's own fuzzy math. For the most part the distribution went smoothly. Gregg continued recording each cop's size and ID badge number and scolded the cops for still carrying the flimsy temporary IDs that had been replaced with sturdier cards.

"I swear we're giving full uniforms to Taliban guys," he said sev-

eral times, only half joking. It wasn't uncommon for equipment to find its way to the market, where it was sold to vendors to supplement a cop or soldier's paycheck.

Matt and Mike handed out the pants and tops. The Afghans tried on the shirts, sometimes letting one sleeve dip way down, making it impossible to see how the shirt really fit. Matt was constantly telling the Afghans that there was no such thing as a custom fit.

"This is not a fucking tailor shop," he said repeatedly.

By the end, most of the small uniforms are gone and the last few Afghans were forced to wear sizes that were too big for them.

"You're going to have to cinch it up with a belt, bro," Matt told them as they complained about the fit.

A couple of the bigger Afghans were too fat to fit even the biggest sizes.

"Take a lap, bro. Skip a meal. That is all we got," Matt barked at them.

After all the cops received their uniforms, it was the officers' turn. Namatullah and others asked for two sets, but were told no by Courtney, who'd found out earlier that day that Namatullah and the other officers had told the cops to refuse to go out on patrol if they didn't get uniforms.

"I had to do some professional development," Courtney told me as I handed out boots. Translation: Namatullah and the boys got their asses chewed.

Before the team left, Matt asked Namatullah for a list of the serial numbers of the unit's rifles and machine guns.

"I will give you the list if you give me another uniform," Namatullah told Matt.

He was not joking.

Days after raging about the corruption of the government,

Namatullah was scheming with the best of them. In Afghanistan, corruption was a subject you railed against only when you weren't getting a taste.

"That is not how it works," Matt said, walking away from the Afghan.

CHAPTER 6

DISTRICT 9

There is no American and very little Afghan presence in Kandahar City's District 9.

Situated in the northern slums of the south's largest city, the district was a bedroom community for the insurgents working in the outlying districts. For the past several weeks, the team and its partner force, the 2nd Battalion, 3rd Afghan National Civil Order Police Brigade, had been setting up checkpoints and patrolling the area before they were pulled into the center of the city for Eid.

The governor of the province, Tooryalai Wesa, wanted the ANCOP in the city to maintain security during the holiday and the upcoming elections. And while the team would have preferred to stay in the district, the ANCOP belonged to the Afghan government and went where they were ordered.

The Afghan National Civil Order Police were created in July 2006 as a crisis and antiterrorist response force. Under the nation's Ministry of the Interior, the ANCOP had more than five thousand officers divided into four brigades in Kabul, Paktia, Kandahar, and Herāt.

Since they went through a full sixteen weeks of training and had a higher literacy rate than the regular Afghan National Police, the ANCOP recruits were generally considered part of a more elite force. The ANCOP was routinely utilized as a replacement force when a local unit of the Afghan police was sent for training near Kabul or as a "surge" force to help secure a troublesome area.

On average, an ANCOP officer deployed for a longer time than his police counterpart, which ended up creating a lot of turnover within the force. ANCOP soldiers were always going AWOL, leaving their posts and taking their weapons with them.

That was one of the reasons why the Green Berets were brought in to mentor the cops. The government needed them to be a success, but the American forces they were partnered with weren't getting it done. Not only did the Special Forces bring advanced training, but they brought a know-how to the job that the conventional units lacked.

The Special Forces were built to train native soldiers, and so far the partnership was working. There was no attrition, and the checkpoints seemed to be keeping security. Only once was the ANCOP attacked. This came days before I joined up with the team, and it was a short ambush. Really, it was just one guy with an AK-47. A little spray-and-pray before hiding in the winding alleys of the district. No one was hurt and the rounds made more noise than anything else.

The only other highlight in recent weeks that I'd missed was the arrest of the District 9 police chief. He tried to get through a checkpoint with a weapon and no ID card. Rules were rules, and the ANCOP detained him. Courtney applauded the ANCOP for it and looked forward to their reestablishing themselves in the area after the holiday.

Since the ANCOP was operating in Kandahar City, the team also had to work with the 4th Infantry Division's 1st Brigade, a conventional unit out of Fort Carson, Colorado.

The 4th ID—as it was called by the soldiers—was based at Camp Nathan Smith, a small base in the eastern part of the city. The base was literally tucked into the city. Jammed with vehicles and buildings, there was a real claustrophobic feeling to the place. And with the 4th ID and several other units, including a civil affairs team and a provisional reconstruction team, at the base, the dining hall was packed.

Standing in a long line that snaked up to the front door of the dining hall, we waited for about a half hour. Once inside, we saw that almost all the tables were packed. The soldiers serving the food almost stopped the Afghan cops at the door. They told Courtney that Afghans couldn't eat at the dining hall—an order the team ignored, ushering them into the main line for food and just staring at the soldiers' weak protests and stern looks.

"This is their country," Matt said as he got a plate.

Excluding Afghans, Iraqis, or any locals from dining halls was common practice. Since an Iraqi suicide bomber killed twenty-two people—including fourteen U.S. soldiers—and wounded sixty-nine in an attack on a mess hall at a U.S. military base near Mosul, Iraq, in 2004, locals were often banned from such places. I recall visiting the base a few months after the explosion and getting a pat-down before going inside. But the ban on locals, backpacks, large bags, and generally anything but an appetite was still in place.

Lunch was short and eaten in silence because the room was so crowded that we were forced to eat at separate tables. I found myself at a table with a bunch of 4th ID soldiers. We all ignored one another and ate quietly. I enjoyed the air-conditioning and ate my chicken, mashed potatoes, and overcooked green beans.

After lunch, I followed Courtney over to the command center. I wanted to get a sense of where we were and what the team's mission was going to be. Plus, I wanted to meet the other American units. I'd had embeds with the 82nd Airborne Division out of Fort Bragg, one of the best conventional units I've ever seen in the field. The times I'd gone with other units paled in comparison. But what made the 82nd great was also what had made them hard to deal with. A paratrooper's ego is bigger than his parachute. No trooper believes in himself more than a guy wearing the red, white, and blue double-A patch of the 82nd. But I guess that kind of grandiosity is needed if you're going to jump out of a plane only to find yourself surrounded by the enemy.

Having been indoctrinated in that culture, I held some of the paratroopers' contempt for nonairborne units, which they called "leg" units. The few that I'd seen in action hadn't been impressive. So, going into the command center, I was already spoiled. The huge egos of the paratroopers had rubbed off on me in the past, and now, with my beard starting to come in, I was beginning to adopt the attitudes of the Special Forces.

The 4th ID's command center—called a TOC or tactical operations center—was in a large warehouse. Inside, they'd constructed a wooden building with handsome stairs and walls made of plywood. The command center had stadium seating all facing a huge monitor. At the center was a live feed from a camera mounted on a blimp that flew over the camp. Imagine the bridge on *Star Trek*'s *Enterprise,* but made of plywood. That is what the TOC was like; it acted as the brain of the unit.

When I covered the invasion of Iraq, the TOC was in a tent on good days and in a truck most of the time. Few of them were built up like the one the 4th ID was using.

Courtney and Tony met with Major Werkheiser, the brigade's

chief of operations. The lanky major led them back to an office where the future-plans cells worked. These guys mapped out the brigade's missions. They were commanded by a short, bald, and stumpy-looking major named Adams, who stood with Courtney by a map of Kandahar tacked to the wall.

Adams was hoping that the team could hook up with the Afghan National Police (ANP) and help train them along with the ANCOP so that when the team left the city in a few weeks, the ANP would be a more competent force. The local police had a terrible reputation in Afghanistan. They were a symbol of the corruption that was plaguing the nation. At checkpoints, they were known to charge a toll. They demanded bribes from people charged with simple infractions, openly stole from residents, and harbored and transported Taliban fighters in their green Ranger trucks.

The captain was receptive to Major Adams's proposal.

"We're getting good feedback from the populace. They prefer the ANCOP to the ANP," Courtney told him.

Both Werkheiser and Adams admitted knowing nothing about the district and hoped that the SF team and ANCOP would be able to root out the insurgents who were living there; but the majors were also hoping that the team might get a sense of what the people thought of Governor Wesa.

"We have no idea how the people feel about us working closely with the governor," Adams said. "Can you guys map the human terrain?"

Governor Wesa had been born in Kandahar Province and had lived in Canada before returning to Afghanistan in 1989. He was known more as an academic than as a politician, and had been appointed to the governorship only because of his close relationship with the Afghan president, Hamid Karzai, who was as corrupt as they come. Not surprisingly, there were questions about Wesa's character.

In May 2010, he was fired from a job he held with a U.S. government contractor after he allegedly used his position with the company to funnel benefits to his family and tribe.

I'd only been on the ground for a few days, but listening to the two 4th ID officers didn't give me a lot of hope about the United States' chances for success in Afghanistan. It was sort of obvious to me that the people were not receptive to the 4th ID's style of counterinsurgency. How did the locals feel about the governor and the government? If Namatullah was any indicator, they felt like they were getting fucked by the government.

And by "hooking their cart up with the governor," who was a pawn of the Karzai family, the Americans were making things worse. With the 4th ID in tow, the governor was, in effect, in possession of a huge goon squad, complete with armored vehicles and the latest technology.

But on the flip side, what was the 4th ID unit supposed to do? They were stuck in a common dilemma that I'd seen play out over and over again on almost every trip. The Americans needed a local partner in order to be effective. Sometimes, the partner was good, like the ANCOP, or the American-trained Afghan commandos, or the Afghan National Army. Sometimes the partner was not so good, as in the case of the ANP; and sometimes the partner was outright corrupt, like the governor.

It all depended on how much corruption was tolerable. And in some ways this was an impossible thing to measure.

As they left the meeting, no one was impressed. Courtney kept quiet, but his body language betrayed his frustration. The lack of a plan and being tethered both to the 4th ID and to the Afghan Ministry of Interior made life difficult.

For me, the meeting was indicative of an overall weakness in the

U.S. strategy in Kandahar. Partly as a result of cultural ignorance, partly as a result of a failure to find a way to use all the units' capabilities on the battlefield, the Army was still in Afghanistan nine years after the war began, still fighting the same fight. The war had turned into an endless circle, and the captain and SF team knew they were stuck on a treadmill.

Back out on the city streets, I finally found myself getting a feel for the place. I'd spent time in southern Afghanistan on past trips, but this was my first time in Kandahar City. I'd only driven through it before, watched it pass by from the inside of a Humvee. Now, though, we were traveling in MRAP armored trucks. The thick plates and V-shaped hull protected the truck's crew from roadside bombs, but the trucks were huge and difficult at times to maneuver in the city's narrow streets.

Riding in the hatch next to the rear gunner, a spot I tried to take as often as possible as we drove, I watched the streets unfold around me. Since MRAPs are so high off the ground, I had a great vantage point and could scan the buildings and see well past the traffic jams that snarled the streets.

A constant hazard was the rock throwing.

"Rocks on your left!" Matt yelled to John, who was standing behind the machine gun in the back of the truck.

I could hear the rocks strike the armor and windows of the truck. One bounced off my helmet. For the most part, they seemed harmless. They were thrown by kids who did it for fun or for mischief. Like throwing snowballs at cars in the winter. You really don't want to hurt anyone and just do it to pass time or on a dare from your friends. At least this is what I thought at first.

These teens, though, could really whip them, I heard Matt say as I ducked down. A rock hit one guy from another team in the helmet and blew out the blood vessels in his eye. By now, Matt was convinced that the kids weren't hurling rocks just for fun. They had an agenda.

"The older ones with the good arms," Matt said. "They're fucking haters."

Some of the kids tried to hit the turret where Matt's camera and gun sat, seemingly in hopes of disabling it. I'd never seen the Afghans so hostile. In 2007, I'd spent a month in Khost in the eastern part of the country. The city, right on the border with Pakistan, was infamous for its suicide bombers. But when I was there, it was relatively safe. I'd spent two days walking in parks and visiting the university and the head of the women's center. I did all of this without having to don body armor and have an Army escort. And the Afghans all greeted me warmly.

But today, as we drove through the city, I didn't feel the same warmth. Granted the east and south were very different places, but the few Afghans I did make eye contact with didn't look at all happy to see me. And the ones who weren't throwing rocks were either ignoring me completely or pretending to shoot me, though none of them actually held a gun.

During the recent holiday celebrations of Eid, though, all the shooting hadn't been make-believe. The kids in the city carried plastic guns—both pistols and AK-47s. The guns were the hot Eid gift and at several stops to check on the ANCOP, kids in the crowd pointed the toy guns at me and the team.

One of our last stops was at a traffic circle on the east side of the city. While the team checked on the Afghans who were engaged in setting up a checkpoint, Ben and I started talking to the kids. It didn't take long for word to get out that we'd stopped, and soon we were surrounded by kids. I looked around to see if any of them was holding a toy gun, which had been the "hot" gift item at Eid that year, and saw a six- or seven-year-old with a small plastic pistol. It took all my charm—and the bribe of a pen, which the kids are fiends for—to coax him into letting me just hold it.

Up close, the gun looked like a cheap plastic toy. But from a distance, the black finish and faux-wood grip looked authentic.

Taking the gun, I held it in my palm while Ben shot photos of it. He wanted good pictures for the Psy Op guys back at Kandahar. They could make leaflets warning the kids to keep the guns away from the soldiers.

Before we left, Matt came up to talk with the kids. Looking at the fake pistol, he told me how a few nights before he'd been at a checkpoint when a kid came up carrying the exact same pistol. It scared the shit out of him and Tron. Matt said he even stepped back and drew his own pistol before realizing that the one the kid was carrying was a toy.

"I drew down on him quick," Matt said. "That shit was scary."

And at night, it could be lethal.

"I bet the Taliban gave the toys to them hoping that we'd shoot some kids," Gregg said, coming over to look at the plastic pistol. "The fuckers."

Matt agreed.

"I don't want to take their toys away, though," he said. "I can't imagine killing a kid just because he was stupid."

CHAPTER 7

ELECTION DAY

The holiday of Eid had passed quietly, so the team was ready for some action during the election.

So was I. My original plan was to spend a few weeks with ODA 7316 and then embed with a team doing Village Stability Operations. That was the mission I'd planned on covering when I arrived because I'd been told that the VSOs were the future of the war.

But because of the importance of the mission, General David Petraeus had banned embeds with VSO teams. So my embed—and the basis of my book—was lost. Instead, I had to adapt, essentially, to the battlefield I was given. Building up the Afghan police force was a mission that was equally vital as the VSOs, and would give me what I needed for my book. So I threw in with Courtney and the team, who were slated to go out to Zhari, a district west of Kandahar City. The district was the home of the Taliban movement and the team expected a fight when they arrived there. The imminent election only increased the likelihood that we would see some action.

Pulling Tony aside, I asked permission to accompany them. I didn't want to try to stick around a team that didn't want me. Tony liked the idea, although he admitted that he hadn't been keen on having me in the first place. He promised to float the idea with the team.

I'd become friends with most of the team, especially Gregg, Matt, Manny, and Josh, and at this point I felt confident that I'd get the thumbs-up. That night, while I was back at Camp Brown, the team discussed my request. No one shared the details of the meeting with me and I never asked. All I knew was that the next day, when I met up with the team for the election mission, I was in.

Moving out at dawn before the polls opened, we made our way through the gates and checkpoints protecting KAF (Kandahar Airfield) and onto the highway leading to Kandahar City. In a few hours, voters were going to elect members of the Wolesi Jirga, the Afghan parliament, from a pool of slightly more than 2,500 candidates— including 405 women.

For the past several days, the team had been in and out of the city overseeing the ANCOP checkpoints. Each time we stopped, I'd looked at the election posters that covered the compound walls and billboards. The candidates ranged from Western-looking men with suits to more traditional-looking Afghans with thick beards. The interesting part for me was the symbols printed on their posters that were used to identify each candidate. For example, one candidate's symbol was a black-and-white silhouette of a camel. Another's was a car. The symbols were for the citizens who couldn't read, which was slightly more than 70 percent of Afghans. Find the symbol on the ballot and you found your candidate.

Today, as we moved closer to the city, I had a weird feeling that something was going to happen. A few hours before, the team's future home, Camp Wilson, was hit by rockets that landed inside the camp's walls. The rockets destroyed a tent nearby the spot where two members of the team overseeing construction of the new camp used to sleep. Kandahar Airfield had also been hit the night before, but the base was so vast that it was unclear to me where the rockets had landed. I only heard the siren.

There was less joking over the radio than I was used to. Less chatter in the trucks. Maybe it was the earliness of the hour, but I didn't think so. Something just felt different. I'm not big on "feelings" and intuitions, but I'd always followed my gut, and after years of traveling back and forth to Iraq and Afghanistan without a scratch, I felt like I was due. My "antiaction powers," so to speak, were legendary. I'd gone on raids where guys guaranteed there would be a fight only to come back to the base without firing a round. I often joked about my antiaction mojo, telling units I'd embedded with that at some point I was due, and when that point came, it would likely be a seventeen-hour gun battle.

Just as the team hit the outskirts of town, I could see two ANCOP soldiers at a checkpoint rushing to their Humvee. Then, over the radio, word came that there had been an explosion nearby.

"An IED," Matt said. An improvised explosive device.

Parking the truck at a corner, Matt positioned the gun down the street, using the camera to zoom into the crowd, searching for Taliban gunmen.

"Anyone who wants to shoot down this intersection is going to have a bad day," he said.

For the next several minutes, the team waited. Courtney called in the explosion to the 4th ID command center at Camp Nathan Smith, while Matt continued to scan the crowd and waited for an ambush or car-bomb explosion.

As the cars and motorcycles approached, the ANCOP shooed them away. Matt, along with Tron, who was riding shotgun, hopped out of the truck, and they led a few ANCOP up the street to examine where the IED exploded. Climbing out of the back of the truck, I followed, while Ben jumped behind the gun and kept watch.

When I got to the bomb site, I was a little underwhelmed.

The bomb was no bigger than a grenade and hadn't injured anyone but a tan cat, which was lying dead in the middle of the street. While Tron took pictures of the site with my camera, the captain and Matt watched as an Afghan bomb disposal team showed up in a black Hilux pickup truck. The head Afghan was dressed in a white *shalwar kameez*, the traditional long shirt and baggy pants called "man-jams" by most soldiers, and a slick, almost shiny blazer. He held a clipboard and several of the numbered plaques you see in evidence photos.

After examining the scene, he started putting down the plaques near the black scorch mark on the street and began to take his own pictures. He toed some of the debris with a black-loafered foot before shooting another photo. Courtney, watching the Afghans work, stood nearby.

"Hey Captain," Matt said. "Move over here."

Matt had retreated a safe distance from the Afghan bomb squad.

"They're walking around there, stepping on shit."

I watched as the man continued to shoot photos and take notes. The Afghans seemed to be stepping all over the scene with little regard for maintaining the purity of evidence or even for the possibility of other bombs.

There had already been nine explosions—thirty-one by mid-morning—in the city, and in the time it took the team to stop and check on one, we'd heard two more loud booms. Governor Wesa's convoy was even hit by a roadside bomb while he was visiting polling sites. No one was injured in the convoy.

The small bomb we'd heard had detonated near an eye hospital and a polling place. Too small to do any real damage, it was a reminder by the Taliban, Matt said.

"Somebody important owns this hospital or works here. They are just sending a message. 'Hey fuck knuckle,'" Matt said. "'We're still here.'"

The night before, the Taliban had sent letters warning the people of Kandahar "not to vote in 'Americanized elections' and [stating] that anyone doing so would be a target," according to the *New York Times*. Al Haj Ahmad Sayid, the commander of Taliban fighters in Kandahar, signed the letters.

Two more explosions rang out, echoing over the city.

"It's going to be like this all day," Courtney said.

"Many booms," said Matt.

The Taliban had stolen two police trucks a few weeks ago, and the team was certain that they'd use the trucks as car bombs during the election.

"They are just trying to keep the people scared," said Tron in his halting English. "We'll probably see a big one around noon."

While some of the explosions were small, others sounded bigger, but all of them rattled the Afghans on the street, who moved with a brisk pace as they walked to work or home.

With the Afghan squad in control, Courtney, Tron, and Matt walked back to the trucks and greeted the Afghans on the street. Courtney even stopped to talk with one onlooker who invited him up to his home for tea. Of course Courtney couldn't go. He had to get to Camp Nathan Smith before the polls opened. American military units were told to keep a low profile during the election in order to give the illusion that it was an Afghan event.

"Are you voting today?" Courtney asked the man, who had a thick black beard and dark eyes.

"After I drink some chai," he said.

I have no idea if he did vote. This was the second election I'd covered and both times I'd heard the same question about going to vote followed by the same answer. Even in the United States, where we don't have to brave bombs in order to get to the polls, we don't vote.

At Nathan Smith, it was business as usual. Soldiers walked around the camp tending to the vehicles in the motor pool. The team parked their trucks in one corner and shed their body armor. While Courtney and Tony headed to the headquarters to check in, Tron and Matt went to the mayor's cell to see about using the shooting range. When Green Berets have downtime, they like to train. And the best training is done on the range.

Matt packed several cans of ammunition and a thick roll of zombie targets. Gregg invited some medics and doctors from the aid station to join in the practice. This was rapport building at its finest: the training invitation got the team an invitation to the med clinic's cookout.

I followed the captain to the headquarters because I was curious about the bombs. At the headquarters, the 4th ID soldiers looked harried. Werkheiser, the brigade's chief of operations, had crazy eyes. He barely looked up as Courtney tried to tell him about the explosion near the hospital. On the big screen at the front of the room, slides flashed and maps showing polling sites filled the walls. Werkheiser had his hands full with the election and sort of nodded through Courtney's report before referring him to another captain a few workstations away. I retreated to the bottom of the TOC floor and stared up at all the feeds and maps. The election was a huge undertaking and impossible to fully protect. I could see why Werkheiser was frazzled. After giving his report, Courtney walked outside into the hall. He seemed annoyed with the treatment he had received.

"I get more response from a five-year-old kid," was his comment.

With nothing left to do but wait for trouble, I headed over to the range. Matt and the rest of the team were getting ready to shoot. The training started with a warm-up of one magazine at fairly close range. Then Matt staggered the targets so that the shooter walked through them, engaging the targets to his left and right.

"I want two in the chest and one in the nugget. I don't want to see any fliers," Matt said.

He urged the team and medics to take their time. Aim. Because with the enemy spraying and praying, a trained American soldier only needs one shot.

"Slow down and make sure everything is perfect."

The Green Berets—who were wearing mullet wigs they'd procured from Mike the Cop—shot first, and the medics watched. It was clear that the team was comfortable with their weapons and seemed to move quickly and smoothly through the maze of targets, their new hairdos flowing behind them. Their shots became a minibeat as each one took his turn: *pop, pop,* then a half-second beat, then another *pop.* Only Josh seemed truly comfortable in the wig, chattering away, his Alabama accent seasoning every word, including several renditions of Lady Gaga's "Poker Face." If he wasn't singing a pop song, he was telling someone to lick his balls.

When the team was done shooting, the medics took their turn. A team member who gently critiqued the medic's form followed close behind.

This kind of mentoring is at the heart of the way Green Berets go about training. They don't dumb it down for the lowest common denominator; instead they take a hands-on approach and act as tutors, working one-on-one. They do this with Afghan soldiers and cops the same way as they were doing it with the medics in the 4th ID.

But before they could finish the training session, the radio crackled.

"Range 1. KPRT. Cease fire."

All the shooting had startled the commanders at the base, and with the election going on, they decided to shut it down. The rest of the morning was boring. I sat in the back of one of the trucks and dozed.

Around lunch, we all joined the medics back at the clinic for kebabs, spicy sausages, and movies. The clinic was set up near the center of the camp. Next to the main treatment room, there was a small lounge with couches and a TV hooked up to an Xbox into which some movies had been downloaded. Crowded on the couches, the team took over the break room and watched *Training Day* and *Boondock Saints* back-to-back. Outside, Gregg and Jake, with Jake's dog, Apollo, talked to the doctors, and Gregg even performed some basic dental work on some troops from the 4th ID.

Around noon, Courtney got called to the headquarters, where he learned that the ANCOP had been ordered to move to Zhari in two days. The captain thought the ANCOP wasn't moving until the first week in October. But a brigade from the 101st Airborne Division needed help. Their base had been rocketed that morning and the unit was taking a lot of casualties. The soldiers were clearing the district, which was home to Mullah Omar, the leader of the Taliban, and needed the police to come in to back them up and hold the ground. The only problem was that the 101st had failed to build a camp for the team or for the ANCOP. So with no place to sleep, eat, or shit, it was impossible to bring almost two hundred ANCOP cops to the district.

The whole affair came down to a pissing contest between the 101st and Special Forces, a lack of planning by the 101st brigade at the base, and an unnecessary burden on the team who would have to make it happen. It was the start of an almost constant stop and go with the 101st. One second the team would prepare for a mission, only to have it yanked back and changed in the next.

"We keep getting a shit sandwich and they keep adding hot sauce to it," Courtney said back at the ODA base near KAF after he unsuccessfully lobbied for more time.

Despite several loud booms, the team stayed at Nathan Smith until the polls closed at 4 P.M. At least fourteen people were killed, and there were reports of bombings and rocket attacks in several cities, including Kabul. Voter turnout was low, with more than 3.5 million out of the 10 million eligible voters actually completing a ballot. The low turnout was credited to the Taliban, who threatened all of the candidates and delivered night letters to voters in Kandahar warning them not to vote.

But the election was far from the members of the team's minds now as they headed back to Kandahar to plan for a trip to Camp Wilson the following day to see what progress had been made on the Special Forces camp, which was being built next to the 101st base. The captain told the team that the 101st was convinced that a Special Forces team would enhance security and help keep the area safer.

"They expect us to work wonders," Tony said.

Manny laughed. At Wilson, Manny was convinced they would need more than mullet wigs on their heads in order to get the job done. They'd seen the camp on a previous trip, and witnessed the mood there. The place had no operating space, and it would be up to the Green Berets to take the fight to the enemy.

"We should get capes to go with our wigs," Manny said.

But Courtney promised the team that no operations would be happening until the camp was built. There wasn't another team in the area and the guys were expected not only to mentor and train the ANCOP cops, but to develop the area for intelligence and try to exploit and target enemy fighters. It was going to be a fight that would challenge them every day. Plus, they were writing the playbook for training and mentoring ANCOP.

And finally, Zhari, birthplace of the Taliban, was one of the most dangerous areas in Kandahar. The 101st unit had already suffered more than thirty casualties, and that wasn't counting the number of wounded.

"At the end of the day," Courtney said, "I want to bring everybody home."

CHAPTER 8

GET YOUR CAPES

The premission briefing for the trip to Camp Wilson began outside the team's operations center.

The team and members of the B-team from the 3rd Special Forces Group, the team's unit that helped with plans and support, milled around in front of the operations center, many of them spitting streams of tobacco into the gravel.

The headquarters driver was late and now the whole plan was in jeopardy.

The Afghan trucker who was supposed to take a pair of generators to the team's new camp hadn't shown up. Dave, the junior engineer on the team, was in charge of logistics and was chain-smoking and barking into his cell phone, trying to track him down. Dave was one of the quietest members of the team, a man who seemed to speak only when spoken to, and this was the most I'd seen him talk since my arrival.

Dave had been working food-service jobs in Maryland after high school when he enlisted in the Army. His family has a long history of military service. His father served in the Army during the Vietnam era and his grandfather was a medic in Korea.

Dave used to play soldier as a kid and always knew that he'd enlist someday. When he finally did, he signed up to be a combat engineer and was assigned to the 3rd ACR (Armored Cavalry Regiment) out of Fort Carson, Colorado. He deployed to Iraq in 2006 before dropping his packet for Special Forces in 2008. After selection, Tony trained him in the qualification course before joining the team. He was its newest member, but he didn't dwell on the fact.

"I don't look at it as being the new guy," he said. "I look at it as still being in the process of building up a reputation."

Meanwhile, the B-team sergeant major was patrolling the area. He was also liberally indulging in his pet peeves—rolled-up sleeves, team patches—which only made the tension worse. Tony told Matt and Gregg to take the patches off in order to placate the sergeant major. They did as he asked, but grumbled about it. To Matt and Gregg, the patches were a symbol of the team and they were proud of wearing them.

The last time the team had gone to Camp Wilson, in the Zhari district, they "made contact," as the phrase goes. *Making contact* is the technical term for getting shot at. The team was driving down Highway One when a few fighters opened fire at their convoy.

Matt was on the gun.

Mike the Cop was on the rear gun.

Grabbing the six-shooter, a grenade launcher resembling a revolver that can fire six grenades in ten seconds, Mike the Cop started lobbing rounds at the compound where the fighters were hiding. As soon as Matt saw the puffs of smoke from the explosions, he opened fire with the .50-cal machine gun. The fighters quickly packed up and escaped down a canal near the compound. A few minutes later, some men popped up out of some brush carrying a wooden box. After burying the box, they disappeared into the thick fields of grapes.

Matt watched them bury the box from behind the gun, but couldn't shoot. He and Mike the Cop weren't able to spot any weapons.

Now, back at Simmons, Courtney began reading off the "con-op," short for concept of operation (every mission has one). The team listened closely. There were no jokes. No wisecracks. Just rapt attention to the details because this time they knew they could be in a fight or get hit by a roadside bomb.

"All of the IEDs are coming out of Zhari," the captain told them.

After the briefing, the team returned to waiting for the Afghan driver. Hours passed until finally Tony gave the order to load up the team's trailers and a flatbed truck parked at the base. I joined the team as they stacked the boxes of kosher meals on the truck. Then Tony took cargo straps and ratcheted them down over the boxes. Rza, the interpreter, was driving the flatbed truck.

It was late morning by the time the convoy raced out of the base and began moving through the city. One day after the election, things were quiet. People shopped at the markets and walked on the street. Near the outskirts of the city, traffic quickly built up. "Jingle" trucks—the name given to the intricately patterned, colorfully painted vehicles with jingling chains and pendants suspended from their front bumpers—were crammed along the shoulders of the road. Afghans mingled along the shoulders, staying in the shade of the trucks. They watched as the team's lumbering trucks rumbled by.

Things got tense when a traffic jam near the bridge over the Arghandab River, along the eastern border of the district, slowed the convoy to a crawl. It was almost claustrophobic with cars pinning the team's trucks in with no way to escape. Soon the Afghan police who were leading the convoy helped push a disabled bus out of the way and the team was racing across the bridge.

On the other side of the river, the Zhari district looked green and lush. Fields of corn, marijuana, and grapes looked like little green patches on a tan blanket. Deep irrigation ditches cut the fields into perfect squares. Occasionally, a massive square grape-drying hut seemed to pop up out of a field. The huts had thick mud walls and were often used by Taliban fighters as weapons caches and ambush sites. Few American weapons were big enough to puncture the walls and the Taliban fighters could fire from holes cut in the walls.

Matt kept a constant watch on the tangle of fields and irrigation ditches off the road, using the camera's zooming power to peek into the grape huts or into windows and doors of the surrounding mud huts. Speed meant safety and the trucks were moving at a good clip. The convoy tried to maintain this speed, but had to stop just past the city when some of the kosher meals for the Afghan police fell off the truck. The straps holding the boxes to the flatbed came undone, and a few of them rolled off the truck and smashed onto the highway.

Tony's truck, which was at the rear of the convoy, had to stop, pick up the boxes, and throw them back onto the trailer.

Sitting in the back of a truck with Matt, I looked out the thick glass window at the sides of the road. The asphalt pavement was rough and pockmarked, with huge holes that were like speed bumps. Each hole was a reminder of the constant threat of roadside bombs. It was a threat that started in Iraq and had only become a huge problem in Afghanistan during the past five years .

I was in Baghdad in 2004, and the soldiers who were stationed there were shocked when the bombs started popping up. I remember interviewing an 82nd Airborne soldier who'd survived the explosion of three of them in one day. At the time the bombs were looked at as a nuisance rather than a major problem. By now, though, insurgents were building bombs that were large enough to disintegrate a Humvee. One, detonated in Iraq, even caused an armored personnel carrier to flip over.

To protect themselves from the bombs, the team drove around in RGs, huge armored trucks with V-shaped hulls that can withstand a blast. But driving around in them felt like being in a spaceship. It was impossible to hear bullets and every time I climbed down from the back of the vehicle, with its massive armored hydraulic door, I felt like Neil Armstrong taking his first step onto the moon.

As Zhari sped by, I felt more like I was watching a *National Geographic* special about the Afghan countryside than actually being in it. I was reminded of a photographer I had worked with, Andrew Craft, who came up with this great feature he called "Humvee TV." He shot photos through the glass of armored Humvees; the images he obtained looked like something you were watching on TV rather than something you had witnessed close up. To me, these images were always a reminder of the distance that separated the American soldiers in their big armored trucks from the people of Afghanistan or Iraq.

The war in Afghanistan was a "people-centric" war; if I felt cut off from the people as I sat in the truck, how, I wondered, would the Afghans be feeling at the other end? One intelligence sergeant told me that Afghans he talked with said Americans are arrogant because of these trucks in which they roared by the population of the towns and villages.

Despite the widespread evidence of IEDs, not to mention the team's last trip to Camp Wilson when they got shot at, the convoy arrived without incident. Somewhat to my chagrin. Of course I didn't want to see anyone hurt, but for the first time I had almost been certain that something was going to happen, and of course it didn't. As I already mentioned, I have a reputation for being something of an "antiaction magnet," which has kept me alive and working in some of the most dangerous areas of both Afghanistan and Iraq, but deep down, a reporter always hopes something will happen that he can write about afterward. It's selfish, for sure. But soldiers feel the same way; they want to see some action too. And they're lying if they say they don't.

This was my first trip to Camp Wilson, which sat right next to the highway. The base was protected by Hesco barriers, wire baskets filled with dirt, and tan guard towers, and the team complained that it was far too close to the highway. From the road, you could see over the walls, to the interior of the camp, which made Matt and the others nervous. What would stop some insurgents from driving by and firing a few rounds or an RPG into the camp?

Rumbling to the team's future base, the trucks pulled into a gravel field with a U-shaped set of containers covered by a green camouflage net. As I pulled off my body armor and helmet, I could hear an irate Tony yelling at the team.

Jumping out of his truck, he began barking for the team to get in formation. I'd been very diligent about helping the team when work needed to be done. At the end of patrols, I helped clean up the trucks and carry machine guns and grenade launchers to the operations center. I'd made it my mission to try to become as much a member of the team as I could, and that included doing the team's work. When I saw the formation, though, I knew that wasn't for the likes of me, so I stayed nearby to hear if Tony was about to deliver some specific directions.

He wasn't.

Once the Green Berets were formed up, Tony ordered them to do push-ups, sit-ups, and leg lifts. He was "smoking" them for being lazy, not paying attention to the other, possibly more pressing matters, and making a mess of the whole convoy to Wilson.

He screamed about the meals falling off the truck. He screamed about the Afghan driver not showing. He screamed about rolled-up sleeves and team patches. Some of the guys had rolled up their sleeves because it was a hundred degrees outside and they were on the rear guns with the sun beating down on them.

But Tony was doing this in front of the B-team and the ANCOP, who stood by uncomfortably. I didn't really know what to do. This kind of chewing out was common in conventional units, like the 101st Airborne and 82nd Airborne, but I had never seen anything like it in a Special Forces team.

The team itself just grunted as they worked through the exercises. But each member had a stern look on his face. The exercise wasn't the punishment. The punishment was the embarrassment they were being forced to endure. They'd been degraded in front of their peers and the men they were supposed to train. Tony was treating them like screwup students, not soldiers who'd passed the qualification course and earned the Special Forces tab.

"It was the most embarrassing moment in my Army career," Gregg said later, his face still flushed with anger.

I'd detected an underlying dislike for Tony since I'd gotten to the team, but this was the first time it had risen to the surface. At first, I figured he was still feeling his way around since this was his first stint as a team sergeant. Let me be clear: I had no idea of how one goes about being a team sergeant. I'd seen good ones and bad ones, but the difference between a successful team and an unsuccessful one was usually tied to the performance of the team sergeant. He was the foundation. He was the man who harnessed all the egos and kept them working toward a common goal.

Born in New York, Tony had moved to Puerto Rico when he was a teenager. He joined the Army as a supply clerk after high school, in 1996, at a time when his English still wasn't good. He didn't really want to work in supply, but the recruiter told him that he could switch

generally catching up since he'd been more or less in exile from the team at Wilson, building the camp. Matt and Manny delivered a sniper rifle, which Mike said he planned to use the next time the camp took fire. A few days before, a rocket had landed near their former tent, setting it on fire. Rockets, mortars, and small-arms fire hit the camp frequently.

Around dinnertime Rick took the team, minus Courtney and Tony, who were still in meetings, to the chow hall.

"They'll be getting their kit on now," Rick said as he walked the team into the center of the camp.

What he was alluding to was the fact that the camp was attacked with rockets at dinnertime every day. So, instead of sending out a patrol or setting up snipers in hopes of catching the shooters, the whole camp put on their helmets and body armor. They also closed the chow hall and everyone had to get "to go" plates so that they could avoid being massed in one location.

To the team, the rules made no sense. We were at war and the soldiers at the camp were infantry. Instead, the soldiers seemed to be content to let the Taliban tell them what to wear to dinner.

"We're not here to shoot people," Manny said in a mocking, high-pitched voice as we walked through the camp. "We're here to make friends. The Taliban are a majestic people. Boo."

As the team walked, without body armor, the other soldiers watched with resentment. A few contractors, in their gear, banged shoulders with Gregg, almost causing a fight. Even the contractors who were serving the food were wearing body armor. They looked shocked to see the team without it.

One officer even called out Matt for his sleeves.

"Hey, you! Special Forces or not, we don't roll our sleeves up around here!" the officer said. He was wearing his helmet, body armor, and goggles.

Since I was with them, without body armor, I got the same nasty looks. It was strange but even I felt a little ashamed. These were members of the 101st Airborne Division, some of the first soldiers into Normandy during D-day. A unit with a distinct combat heritage in Vietnam and in the invasion of Iraq, and here they were, cowering at Camp Wilson. But I know what the soldiers were thinking. And Gregg put it best. He said that there were only two ways that conventional soldiers treated a Special Forces team.

"They hang on every word or they are straight haters," he said.

The Special Forces team was flaunting the fact that they weren't wearing body armor. It also sent a message. The team was at Wilson to fight and they were different than the conventional units.

As we walked back to camp with our food, Gregg looked around with disgust. We were surrounded by soldiers in full kit huddled in concrete bunkers eating their steak and lobster tails. It made him sick. Gregg understood that the soldiers were just following their officers' orders; he understood that their situation was unlike the situation of the team, and that for them to ask why and challenge the logic of certain orders was not something that went over well. He figured the 101st soldiers wanted to go and fight too, and he blamed their officers, like the one who had yelled at Matt, for not leading.

"They need to tell their commanders they want to fight instead of counting down the days before they can go home," Gregg said, adding, "Dick Winters would have butt-stroked someone."

I doubted any of the soldiers deployed to Afghanistan to eat lobster in a bunker. The problem was the war had matured so bureaucracy replaced initiative. Everything was scheduled with at least an hour of mandatory pre-patrol checks including making sure every soldier had proper eye protection. And if they did go out and patrol, who was going to stay behind to answer all the e-mails coming from the headquarters?

The infantry exists to fight the enemy, but combine the bureaucracy with the frustration of a seemingly invisible but fully capable enemy and it looked like we were beating ourselves.

Back at their camp, the team crowded around a worktable and ate their dinner. No one liked what they saw, but all seemed eager to move and get into the fight. It was clear in just one short walk to the chow hall that Camp Wilson needed the Special Forces.

"We're going to be supermen. We're going to get out there and take the enemy out of its comfort zone. People are too cautious. We're going to take it to them and we're going to kill them first," Manny said. "We better bring our capes."

After an uneventful ride back to Simmons, the team met again in front of the operations center. Again, Tony blasted them for their poor performance and called out Gregg and Matt again for rolling up their sleeves and wearing a team patch. The mood was tense and you could see the anger on the men's faces as they clenched their jaws and looked away from Tony. As soon as the meeting was over, the team broke up without a word.

No jokes from Josh.

Nothing.

This was a whole new territory for Courtney, who admitted that it was a little intimidating for him to walk into the team room the first time. He knew most of the guys had more experience in Special Forces than he did. He knew that they were the experts in their fields. Rick had more time in Special Forces than he himself had in the Army.

"But you've got to go into the team room," the captain had said a few days earlier. "You've been assigned to the team."

It was his team room now. But, he told the guys, he was relying on them to teach him as much as possible.

He said it helped that Tony was new to the team too. They could work together to set the tone for the team. But he understood that unlike a platoon leader, he had to deal with eleven other type A personalities and find a way to lead each one.

After retreating briefly to their rooms, the team got together and had a closed-door meeting in the operations center. I left soon after this and returned to Kandahar Airfield. But I found out later that the message the team had decided to deliver was a simple one. They were about to move into one of the most dangerous districts in Kandahar and they didn't need the kind of unprofessional behavior and leadership Tony had demonstrated. That was the kind of stuff that got people killed.

"We can't take this attitude to Zhari," was Courtney's message.

I found out that Tony later apologized to the team and to the Afghans who had seen his display of temper. He was close to losing his job after several of the senior members of the team said they'd request transfers to the B-team if things continued the way they were going. For the next several days, Tony treaded lightly. As one team member put it, he was searching for the thick ice again after stepping out way too far on a thin sheet.

Manny, who'd been a really calming influence at Wilson, said the apology was a good first step.

"I hate to see people fail," Manny said. "I think he has handled it well since then. I hope this never happens again. I think Tony is a good guy."

CHAPTER 9

NASHVILLE

While the team got ready to move, a sister team was gearing up for a commando mission.

They'd arrived a few days before with their commando unit and were scheduled for a "hit" in Zhari near Camp Wilson in a couple of nights. Since the operation was big, they'd asked Tony and Courtney for a little help. Tony had given them Gregg, Matt, and Josh. I'd tried to get on as well, but the team sergeant said no.

"You can't write a story if you're dead," he told me.

While Gregg, Matt, and Josh prepped for the mission, the rest of the team got ready for an inspection of sorts.

Lieutenant Colonel Chris Riga, the Special Forces battalion commander, wanted to go out and see the ANCOP in action. Since the election, they'd taken up checkpoints in District 9 again. The night of the sister team's mission, I met up with Courtney at the operations center. Since I couldn't participate in it, I opted to join him in the

B-team's operations center to watch the mission on the Predator feeds. And then at dawn, I'd go out to the checkpoints with the rest of the team.

Before the mission got under way, I spotted Gregg near the gate. He was excited about the prospect of finally seeing some action. This was really his first major combat mission. That was why he was in Afghanistan. He believed in the mission, and he wanted to see some action.

In a TuffBox under his bed, he had dozens of books about war and adventure, and you'll recall that he was the one who selected the Cormac McCarthy quote for the team shirt. I got a sense that Gregg divided the world into two camps—warriors and everybody else. And Gregg saw himself firmly in the warrior camp, part of a long line of men willing to put their lives on the line. Essentially, it was that willingness that pushed him into the Special Forces when he was a bartender in New York and later Chicago.

He needed more action.

"I've got the warrior blood pumping through my veins," he said. "Firefighters, cops, and military guys didn't have to pay for drinks at my bar."

He decided to apply for a job with the fire department in Madison, Wisconsin, and made a deal with himself. If he didn't get the job, he'd join the Army or the Marines.

"I knew it was an itch I needed to scratch," he told me a few days before the mission. "I knew if I didn't do it, I would regret it."

There were over a thousand applications and Gregg made it to the final thirty, but didn't get selected after the interview with the fire chief. So he started looking at the Army and the Marines. He compared benefits and decided to either join the X-Ray program and become a Special Forces medic or go be a Marine officer.

When he went to visit the Marine recruiter, he asked about benefits and other perks. The recruiter, a ramrod-straight Marine with a tight crew cut, told Gregg the Marines didn't have the same kinds of programs as the Army, only the pride of being a Marine.

"That Jedi mind trick didn't work on me," Gregg said.

So, he returned to the Army recruiter and signed up as an X-Ray. He left two days after Christmas in 2005 and began training after the New Year. And five years later, he was getting ready to board a helicopter.

I didn't see Matt, but nearby I saw Josh. He was always the joker, with a warm smile and a loud boisterous greeting, but now he seemed a little subdued. They'd been practicing the raid and were expecting lots of IEDs and Taliban fighters. Josh admitted that the rehearsals with the Afghan commandos could have gone better. It was hard for the Afghan commandos to imagine a target when it was drawn out on the ground or represented by a model on a sand table.

"They can't visualize," Josh said. "Rehearsals are always a disaster."

And after the intelligence brief, they both expected the worst. The 101st said there was an "impenetrable IED belt" between the highway and the target compound. The threat of the bombs made it difficult for the soldiers to have a meaningful presence in the village.

"Getting the IED brief was always tough," Gregg said. "You feel like we're all going to die."

Plus, they told me that the 101st had dropped leaflets in the area warning women and children to stay indoors. The leaflet was a sure tip to the Taliban leaders to leave the area and to the fighters to hide their weapons.

"It probably won't be anything," Josh said.

A few hours later, I found a seat near the back wall of the operations center. There were two flat-screen TVs, on each of which a very different kind of fighting was taking place. On the screen to the left, North Carolina State's football team was beating Georgia Tech in Atlanta. On the right, the Predator feed showing the team's target—code-named Nashville—filled the screen.

My brother played football for NC State and I'd spent the last four years going to as many games as I could. I rarely missed a home game and made several away games and bowl games. That was the main drawback of coming over to Afghanistan in the fall. I'd miss most of his season. So, being able to watch the game was a real treat. At the time the Wolfpack was undefeated, but Georgia Tech was their first big test.

I kept one eye on the game, especially noting the touchdowns, because my brother was the long snapper on the extra-point and field-goal teams. Between checks of the score, I focused on the black-and-white monitor on the right side of the room. I could just make out an Afghan compound. Then the camera would shift to an open field near the village. The field and the compound looked deserted, but I wasn't sure if they really were, because the angle was too wide; I also wondered if they'd been abandoned as a result of the leaflet drop. The Predator was flying circles over the compound, looking for movement.

Nothing.

On the other screen, Wolfpack's quarterback, Russell Wilson, methodically marched the offense down the field, ending with a thirty-five-yard field goal. Focused on the game, I saw my brother snap a bullet back to the holder and then watched the ball sail through the uprights.

"One minute," someone called out, and all my attention shifted to the Predator feed.

Two Chinooks suddenly shot out of the left side of the screen, their rotors kicking up a pillow of dust. They quickly descended into a field and I saw small, ant-size soldiers, racing off the back tailgate. Seconds later, the helicopters leaped into the sky and raced offscreen.

"These guys are in for a rude awakening," said another soldier watching the raid.

The room was crowded with members of the B-team. Some were working the night shift. Others were just watching the Predator feed. The captain and Tony didn't say much. The Predator feed quickly shifted from the landing zone to the surrounding compounds, searching for any sign of attack.

Back to the game. With North Carolina leading 10–7, Wilson threw what looked like a touchdown pass to Steven Howard, but it was ruled an incomplete pass. I almost jumped out of my seat when I saw the replay. But a review reversed the call. It *was* a touchdown, and another perfect snap put the Wolfpack up 17–7 at halftime.

On the other screen, the Predator scanned the target compounds. I could see that the soldiers were in a single-file line and marching toward the compounds. Every once in a while, the radio in the back of the room would burst to life.

"Skull 15. Desert Eagle 33."

"Roger, Skull 15."

The team did find one IED in the first compound and I heard some chatter to the effect that the enemy was planning to attack from the south. Matt told me later that he felt really comfortable about going in at night. The chances of getting hit during the march in were very small, and by the time morning came, the team and the Afghan commandos would already be dug in.

As they moved forward, Taliban fighters started talking on their radios. The signals were intercepted by the team and the interpreters translated.

"Hey man, there are people at our grid talking about an ambush,"

Matt remembered hearing. "They can see us moving east to west in a particular field."

A few days after the mission, I interviewed the three team members who had participated in it, since I'd left the operations center soon after they landed. I had to be up early to go on patrol. So, while I slept in Josh and Manny's empty room, they were freezing their butts off in the Zhari district.

All three said the forty-minute helicopter ride in was awful. The helicopters were jammed, and when they finally stood up after sitting on their legs and feet for so long, some of them had lost circulation and just fell over.

"I felt like a drunken fucking sailor," Gregg said.

Added Matt: "That was what I was worried about. I have to stand up in front of forty-five commandos and not fall on my ass. I need to look like I know what the hell I am doing."

Finally on the ground, Matt and his commandos were about two hundred meters north of the spot where they wanted to enter the village. Farther south, Josh and Gregg's group blew a hole in the wall of one compound and quickly started to clear the room. All they found were women, children, and goats.

It was the same for Matt.

"Our compound 'mazed out' real quick. It ended up being three buildings that were all connected by hallway tunnels," he said. "We had thirty males on my side. We had stupid amounts of women and children. They didn't put up a lot of resistance and most of them had a look like 'I hope to God he doesn't find out where I hid my stuff.' They had that look in their eye like shit."

The rest of the night, they set up and waited for morning. And pretty much froze to death until the morning came. Matt ended up staying up all night because it was only him and five commandos in his corner of the compound.

"I wasn't about to fall asleep and be like yeah, I trust you guys to pull security," Matt said.

Josh and Gregg set up across town.

"It was the town shitter. They love to shit inside those buildings," Gregg said. "There were random walls, and the walls that had the best shade over the course of the day, they would poop along those too."

As soon as the sun came up, things picked up. An A-10 came in low over the village. Matt thought it was going to be a show of force—essentially flying low and loud—but it opened fire down the road. Shell casings were bouncing into the compound.

"It was close. It was really close. We were pulling guys off the wall," Matt said.

The same thing happened to Gregg and Josh. All Josh could do was pray that the pilot didn't overshoot. It was that close.

The relief force of 101st soldiers arrived just after sunrise. They were smoked, and collapsed in the compound when they arrived. They were supposed to arrive at 2 A.M., but they ended up getting there at five-thirty because they picked a terrible route. They decided to move through the grape fields, which forced them to climb over wall after wall. Their packs were so heavy that it took a long time for the soldiers to cross the fields.

While the 101st soldiers rested, the commandos kept a constant watch. Unlike patrols in the city, the rules of engagement were less restrictive here.

"We didn't need a lot of permission to do a lot of stuff. We knew that we were going into a hostile environment. We knew that the military-aged males were going to be fucking bad dudes," Josh said. "We had a road going east to west. If a fucker came by on a motorcycle, they were lighting them up."

On Matt's side of the village, there was a pudgy man with a thick beard wearing a white scarf and blue *shalwar kameez* standing on a rooftop watching them. Matt had him in his sights when the man took out a phone.

Okay, you're not calling anybody, buddy, Matt thought as he squeezed the trigger.

The Afghan spotter didn't finish keying in the number. Matt shot him in the leg and he fell off the rooftop. I don't know what happened to him after that.

"He didn't fall gracefully," Matt said.

A little while later, the guns at Camp Wilson started shooting artillery near the compounds. One round hit near Matt. He was stunned, but not hurt; the round luckily was a dud or he'd have been killed. That night, as the guns continued to pound the area around them, the commandos and Special Forces soldiers marched out before grabbing helicopters back to Camp Simmons.

So much for that "impenetrable IED belt" and all the fighters hiding in the village.

CHAPTER 10

SF STUFF

It was just after dawn when our convoy snaked out onto the main road heading to Kandahar City.

The two-lane paved road that runs from the center of town to the airport and then to the Pakistani border was packed with Japanese sedans, large Mercedes trucks, and Toyota 4x4 pickups. All of the cars looked beat-up, dented, and dusty. Most of the trucks were painted with garish designs and had charms and ornaments hanging from chains.

Sitting in the back hatch, I could see the trucks cautiously moving behind the convoy. As we got closer to the city, motorcycles joined the melee, darting between the cars. Donkey carts loaded down with wheat from the nearby farms competed with the cars for space on the shoulder of the road.

Kandahar had an awful smell—like something was burning—and the stink hung over the city for most of the day. Passing a traffic circle, the team headed north toward District 9. Their ANCOP partners were manning checkpoints along a canal that separated the district from the rest of the city. It was the proverbial railroad track.

While Matt, Gregg, and Josh were in Zhari with the commandos, the rest of the team was in the city inspecting the checkpoints before Lieutenant Colonel Riga arrived later that morning to see the ANCOP in action.

The canal was little more than a trickle of water, brown and muddy. Trash littered the bank and there was a sheen to the water from sewage or fuel. An old Afghan man, his beard streaked with dust, squatted near one of the footbridges washing his clothes.

As the team drove by, the children threw rocks. Even a pair of young girls, dressed in sparkling red-and-green dresses, threw a few pebbles. One kid ran out after the last truck passed and threw a baseball-size stone that hit the bullet-resistant glass a few inches from my opened hatch.

"Hey," screamed Mike the Cop, who was on the gun next to me. He shot the kids his best "cop" scowl as the truck drove off. But what was he going to do, shoot the kid? The rock throwing was a perfect protest, a hostile act for which there was no possible reprisals. Mike the Cop said he'd seen adults urge their kids to throw rocks at the trucks.

A civilian contractor assigned to the team, Mike the Cop had grown up in a family of policemen. His father was one. So were his uncles and their kids. There seemed to be something in his family's blood that drew them to the law enforcement community. So after serving in the Marines, Mike took a job working narcotics in Georgia and eventually moved to Wilmington, North Carolina. On loan from the Marine special operations unit in Herāt, Mike the Cop was the expert on police skills and gave the team some forensic and investigative capability.

When the team reached the checkpoints, they helped the Afghans set up cones and attached mirrors to sticks that could be used to see under cars. Fighters were known to sleep in the district and then cross the canal to plant roadside bombs or carry out attacks in the area surrounding the city. So, the team set the checkpoints along the bridges in hopes of at least slowing the fighters' movement.

As they inspected the checkpoints, I watched the local people. Almost all the Afghans were either friendly or indifferent. There were few hateful looks, like those that we had seen in Zhari. As we walked, Tron told me that his sources were saying that the people liked the ANCOP because they felt safe, and appreciated that the soldiers didn't charge a fee to pass the checkpoint.

Like Tony, Tron had started off as a supply sergeant. Lean and dark with a jet-black mustache, he enlisted and was sent to Germany. When it was time to reenlist, he requested jump school and got it. After earning his wings, he was transferred to Fort Bragg, North Carolina, and the 82nd Airborne. There, he started to take an interest in Special Forces.

A Mexican citizen at the time, he couldn't join Special Forces until he became an American citizen. In 2000, he was selected, but had to wait two years for his citizenship before he could start training. He was trained in communications and graduated the course in 2003. After a brief detour as a trainer, he joined 7th Group.

Now, in Kandahar, as was the case with any stop, the neighborhood kids were soon crowding around the soldiers demanding gifts.

I stuck with Tron as he worked the crowd and played with the kids.

"We could make this whole city happy with just pens and water," Tron said. The kids had no shame and reached for the pen in my hand and the one in my pocket. I beat a hasty retreat to the truck and let the kids badger Tron and the others.

At the truck, Jeremy, the team's junior medic, was trying to treat a kid who'd been struck in the head. He had a huge welt and some swelling. With Gregg gone, Jeremy was the only medic. Nicknamed "Lump," he was a massive human with thick arms and a huge muscular chest. He kept his hair short, which only drew attention to his forehead and the strange way his eyebrows coiled into a snake like an *S* over his eyes. It looked like he was really thinking when he looked at you with those brows.

Jeremy enlisted in the Army when he was nineteen years old as an X-ray tech and completed eighteen months of training before eventually arriving at the 101st Airborne Division based at Fort Campbell, Kentucky. There, he did little X-ray work. Instead, he spent time in the motor pool changing tires; his unit was meant to provide medical care overseas, and didn't really have a mission at home. It pissed Jeremy off that he'd spent more than a year training to do a job that he was never getting the chance to do.

In 2005, his unit deployed to Iraq. Sent to a sprawling base near Saddam's hometown of Tikrīt, he finally started working as an X-ray tech. He spent several months in nearby Baiji, where he worked on the growing number of casualties. But after a while, things slowed down and he went back to the routine boredom of war. He essentially spent a year doing what was known as "bitch work," and X-raying soldiers with sprained ankles from jogging on the gravel.

It was then he decided to put in his packet for Special Forces selection. When he finally got back to Fort Bragg for selection, Jeremy knew he wasn't going back to the 101st again. There was no doubt he was going to get selected.

"It's all about how you think when you are sucking and if you are a quitter," he said. "They want to see how you perform under pressure."

He'd requested Special Forces medic because of his X-ray–tech background, and got it. He was assigned to the team in March 2010.

Joining the team was like joining any other unit in the Army. He got to the team room, kept his mouth shut and his head down, and tried to learn from the senior members.

But the biggest difference between being in a conventional unit like the 101st and being a part of Special Forces was living under big-boy rules. On a team, you do your job well and stay motivated and you survive. No one is expected to tell you what to do or how to do it all the time, especially if it is in your specialty.

"The way we think can't work on the conventional side," Jeremy said. "We focus on our readiness. We're always prepared. We don't have time to worry about if our boots are bloused or if we shaved."

And to be honest, no one cares on a team. The focus is always on the mission.

"Big-boy rules is kind of a privilege," Jeremy said. "As long as you get what you need done and you do it right."

It was at the demolition range before the team left for Afghanistan that Jeremy got his nickname, "Lump." Only Courtney called him by his first name. The rest of the team referred to him as Lump or Lumpy because during the practice, Manny said he'd hide "behind the lump here," and the name stuck.

It was a funny name for someone like Jeremy, because being a medic, he was one of the smartest team members and knew more medicine than most medics. He was also one of the most unconventional thinkers on the team. His new apartment in Fayetteville had water bugs—cockroaches anywhere else in the world but the South. The bugs hadn't been a problem at his old place. Remembering two toads that lived at his old apartment, he brought them to his new place. He no longer had any problems with bugs.

But for all his smarts, Jeremy had the strangest tattoos on the team. On his pelvis, just below his belt line, was "José," a three-inch Mexican gardener tattooed over his pubic hair. Wearing a green

T-shirt, cuffed jeans, and a red sombrero, "José" is holding a Toro weed eater. Jeremy jokes often that his Mexican gardener is lazy and his pubes need a grooming.

As Jeremy treated the boy with the head wound, I stood by the rear hatch and watched the Afghans who walked by, many of them poking their heads into the row of shops that lined the canal.

Nearby, two women dressed in burkas walked by, moving through the crowd like ghosts. The children and men paid them no attention. As they got close, I could make out the faint outline of their faces, but nothing more. It was strange to me that so much beauty was covered up in Afghanistan, leaving only the dust and the smell.

But on the flip side, imagine the allure. Since you don't know what "she" really looks like, I am sure that when an Afghan sees a burka-clad woman, his mind conjures up some of the most beautiful women in the world. There was a running joke in both Iraq and Afghanistan that Muslim porn is all wrists and ankles. But while the mind can surely create beauty queens under the burka, I am sure that in reality they look more like the women in the Woody Woodpecker cartoons. You know—the ones you see when Woody lifts the veil of the belly dancer only to see her snaggly teeth.

At each of the checkpoints, the team made corrections. The ANCOP were becoming more competent, but they were still way too lax. Some of the police were not carrying weapons and they were not searching every car or person crossing the canal. When the time came for them to move out to Zhari, that kind of sloppiness might get them killed.

At the final checkpoint, Courtney watched a few cars and motor-cycles pass without a search. He grabbed Rza and the checkpoint commander, a smallish Afghan with sunglasses and a low-slung hol-stered pistol.

"He needs to be searching vehicles. All of his guys need to have at least a pistol or their AK. What happens if we take contact?" Courtney said, showing a little bit of stress but keeping his voice even. "His boss is coming and my boss is coming, so they better look good."

Riga finally arrived and was met by Courtney and the ANCOP commander. Lieutenant Colonel Agha, a slight man with a trimmed gray mustache and deep, calm eyes, shook Riga's hand.

Agha didn't look like much. He was a slim forty-seven-year-old man who looked more Iraqi than the usually weathered and bearded Afghans. But his looks belied his toughness. The lifelong policeman had been shot several times and beaten almost to death by the Taliban.

Using Habib as a translator, the two colonels started exchanging pleasantries that soon became a tug-of-war over who was responsible for the success of the ANCOP in Kandahar City as each man tried to outdo the other in deference and modesty.

"The ANCOP is doing a great, great job," Riga said. "We learn more from you and your men than we'll ever teach you. And we appreciate that."

But the ANCOP colonel smiled and waved off the compliment, putting it back on the training his men had received from the Special Forces.

"For us to be successful, we need to cooperate with each other. And that is what we're doing," Agha said.

"The people are happy with the ANCOP," Riga said, adding that the ANCOP cops were becoming the best police force in Afghanistan. "We're proud to serve with you."

But the Afghan colonel turned the spotlight back on Riga and the team.

"It is Special Forces that made us the best," he said.

But Riga was determined to put the credit back on the ANCOP because Special Forces works by, with, and through their partner force.

"The two are always together and that is what makes us strong," Riga said. "We're brothers. That is why we wear the same uniform."

Both the ANCOP and the team wear the same tan digital camouflage pattern. The team also wore an Afghan flag patch and an ANCOP unit patch like the soldiers.

The exchange went on like that for several minutes, and just when it would seem to be tapering off, it would start again. Agha was no stranger to partnering with other armies. He joined the Afghan police in 1983 and had worked for the Russians, then for the mujahideen, the Americans, and now the Afghan government again. But who his boss was, was never really important to Agha.

It was always about the job.

"My purpose has always been to protect as many people in Afghanistan as I can," he told me.

Married with six children, he still lived in the Parwan Province home his father built and died in near Bagram Airfield. Despite the fact that Agha was based in Herāt, his family still lived in the home.

When the Taliban took over in 1996, they treated Agha and the other inhabitants of his village well for two weeks, then forced them out of their homes and subjected them to their draconian rules, which included the banning of music and photographs, both of which, they claimed, were against Islamic law. Anyone who resisted was beaten.

"It is very offensive to force an Afghan citizen out of their home without their consent," he explained.

Agha fought with the Soviets and worked for the mujahideen— he was even wounded by an RPG fired by one of the latter's fighters—

but he couldn't work with the Taliban. He resisted their authority, gathered together with other policemen, and joined the fight against the Taliban on the side of the Northern Alliance until the Americans arrived.

When Karzai took over, he was promoted to police lieutenant colonel in the police and later took over battalion command in the ANCOP.

With the pleasantries done, Riga led the command party to a small shop. Taking off his helmet, he sat out front chatting with the owner. They began talking about the ANCOP, which the shop owner, a tall Afghan with a thick salt-and-pepper beard, praised.

"They are good soldiers," he told Riga, who had shed his gloves and sunglasses. "They treat people nicely and fair."

"It is good that there are a lot of people outside," Riga said, gesturing to the shoppers in the market. The shop owner agreed. He owned a small stall that sold soft drinks, some canned goods, and other household items.

Soon, chairs were brought around for the captain and the ANCOP commander, steaming-hot tea was served, and the shop owner passed around a bag of sweets. Riga and Courtney each took one before the captain started passing them out to some children who were gathered nearby.

"Is this the best tea in Kandahar?" Riga teased the shopkeeper.

"It is Kandahar tea," the shopkeeper replied.

"It is very good," Riga said, taking another sip from his glass.

Riga told the shopkeeper that he liked Kandahar and appreciated the hospitality he'd been shown.

"Kandaharis are very brave and very hospitable," the shopkeeper said.

Riga nodded.

"They are good people," he said. "We appreciate the people of Kandahar taking care of all of us. I am very happy to see how well your shop is doing, and the bazaar, and seeing all the people outside."

An elder from the neighborhood joined the meeting and told Riga about some of the local road projects. He also told Riga that the area needed a school and a new mosque. Riga asked the elder if the contractors were hiring local labor and the elder said yes.

"That is good," he said, looking at the shopkeeper, "so they can spend their money at this shop."

That drew a chuckle from the shopkeeper.

At one point, Riga leaned over to say something to the captain. You could tell that Riga was in his element, mixing with the people and doing some of the same things he did as a team leader.

"Don't you love this shit?" he whispered to Courtney.

"Yeah," Courtney said.

"And you're getting paid for it."

At that moment the captain, Riga, and the others were actually doing their jobs. It was true rapport building, something I would see Courtney try to do over and over again during later missions, sometimes with mixed results. While Courtney seemed determined to build rapport with the Afghans, other teams often didn't. And hadn't done it for years until they were forced into the villages. Special Forces teams were not getting out enough. Not talking to and mixing with people.

After the meeting, Riga and I walked along the canal between the checkpoints. I'd met him in 2004 and lived near his headquarters on Kandahar Airfield. I wouldn't say that he and I were friends, though we had several friends in common, but we'd crossed paths a few times and I respected him. And many of my friends who knew him respected him as one of the best commanders in Special Forces. He was old school and unconventional, and didn't want the U.S. troops to fight the war as a group of light infantry rolling around the countryside in massive armored trucks. He wanted his teams to go out among the people, to build the relationships he believed needed to be built, not only to find the enemy but to create a nation.

"We really shouldn't be wearing a uniform," he said. "Instead, we should spend the day in civilian clothes driving around the city in a truck meeting with the people."

Riga's point was simple.

Special Forces is people-centric, but the threat of IEDs and the restrictions that were being enforced by conventional commanders were limiting a team's ability to do operations outside of the conventional box. Often, teams were having to act like little infantry units, and the strengths of a team were not being utilized. Just as often, teams were focused on commando missions, which led to their participation in too many raids.

You can't shoot your way to stability.

The Taliban was able to rise to power in part because they offered the people a system of justice. More care had to be given to bridging the gap that yawned between the people and the government, a role the ANCOP could play by providing security.

That was what Riga hoped the ANCOP would do in Zhari, just as they had started to do in Kandahar City.

CHAPTER 11

BOO-BOO LIPS

The move to Zhari was delayed for weeks while the camp was built, and the team started to train the ANCOP for what they believed would be a dangerous mission.

Unlike the conventional units that had previously tried to train the ANCOP, Special Forces focused on more hands-on tutoring. There was no such thing as one-size-fits-all training. Just a gentle hand guiding the Afghans.

The team's first mission was to get the police motivated, equipped, and trained—because they were not going to be taking on petty criminals. They would be taking on trained fighters with AK-47 rifles, RPGs, and machine guns.

And the threat in Zhari was especially high.

"We've got to go out there and do work," Josh said. "There are a lot of shitheads out there."

It was a few days after Matt, Gregg, and Josh's return to the team after the commando mission, and they knew how dangerous the area was. They knew the ANCOP needed the training because the level of violence where they were going was much worse than anything they'd experienced in District 9.

Jammed with the team members in a van, I was headed to the ANCOP barracks to watch the team train the Afghans on movement under fire. Essentially, how to crawl properly. This wasn't the first time the team had trained them on this, so it would be more of a refresher. Teams were constantly training and retraining. That—the need for retraining, I mean—was sort of the frustration that was inherent in working with indigenous troops in general and with Afghans in particular. Oftentimes, it took multiple sessions before any training would stick.

One of the problems with mentoring the ANCOP was the mindset. They were police and were used to taking a defensive posture.

"We're going to go in and try to hold something that has already been cleared," Josh said. "We're stuck going to sit on a checkpoint and wait to get shot at. We're going to have to be offensive if we want to survive out there."

When the team arrived, the ANCOP were in formation waiting. It was a pleasant surprise for the team. Colonel Agha, the ANCOP commander, was in attendance, and was clearly excited about the upcoming training. He knew that when troops were bored, there was going to be trouble. So, as they prepared to move out to the Zhari district, he welcomed the chance to get his men trained up.

Gathering the Afghan police around, Matt started to explain the day's exercises. Essentially, the team wanted to make sure the Afghan police knew what to do when they get shot at because it was certain that the insurgents would test them once they got into the district.

"We're going to get dirty. This is not a punishment. We are teaching you things that will save your lives down the road," Matt said.

Rza, standing nearby, translated.

The first exercise was a low crawl. Manny volunteered to demonstrate. Laying his head in the dust, he crawled low to the ground, only raising his head a few times to see where he was going.

Matt provided commentary as Manny crawled.

"His chest is touching the ground. His head is touching the ground. He extends his right arm and brings his leg up and just shimmies along the ground."

When Manny finally stood up after crawling about twenty meters, his face and beard were covered in dust. The Afghans took one look at how dirty he was and the excuses started pouring out of their mouths.

We only have one uniform. Some of us have allergies.

But after some cajoling, most of them compliantly broke up into six lines and started crawling. The team watched each line, offering tips as they crawled.

"Come on. Let's go, brother. One side, face to the ground."

"Za, za, za." Essentially, "go."

"Bang, bang, bang. Head down. Head down."

Rza and Habib, the team's interpreters, did their best to translate on the fly. Habib was the more vocal, yelling at the ANCOP to move. Gregg stood over one Afghan whose butt was sticking up in the air. He called Rza over to translate for him.

"Tell him he is going to get his sweet little ass shot off if he keeps going high like that."

While most of the enlisted police crawled in the dust, the Afghan officers stood off to the side watching. Courtney saw them and had Rza gather them around.

Courtney was angry. It was typical for the Afghan officers to stand around and let their men do the dirty work. Shedding his uniform shirt and hat, Courtney berated them.

"The reason why we are doing this is to save your fucking lives," Courtney said sternly. "When we go to Zhari and the bullets start flying, we're going to have to medevac your fucking bodies out."

While the Afghan soldiers watched, Courtney squatted to the ground then started to crawl. Soon the Afghan officers joined him and the men started to cheer. Other team members got down and began to crawl too. It quickly turned into a race. Courtney finished first. Popping up in a cloud of dust, he returned a high five from Manny as he cleaned off his face.

The training continued from there with a high crawl—using your legs and elbows to move—and then moved on to "rushes" and finally "buddy rushes." The rushes involved a sprint followed by a dive to the ground.

"You do it with two people so that your buddy can cover you," Matt explained when the session had moved on to the buddy rushes. "The first guy goes and starts firing. Three seconds and the next guy goes. Stop, set up, and yell 'set.' Then your buddy goes. Make sure you don't run in front of the other guy."

The team and ANCOP did the rest of the training together, including working in buddy teams with Americans covering Afghans and vice versa. By the time they got to buddy rushes, the Afghans were cheering and training with gusto. Every man, American and Afghan alike, was covered in dust.

At the end, Matt gathered the Afghans together again.

"That shit sucks. That shit is hard. It is not fun at all. But the guys here, they are going to remember your faces and names. Working hard in training leads to missions. Of the two hundred ANCOP guys we have here, you are the best ones. We'll use you the most because you are motivated," Matt said. "No joke. This will save your life. We're proud of you guys. That was a good day of training."

Agha spoke next. He applauded his men for their hard work.

"We have a serious fight in Zhari," he said. "This will keep you alive."

A few days later, the team showed up again to train. Matt, Gregg, and Jeremy, the team's junior medic, were there to teach the ANCOP how to react to fire at a checkpoint.

But none of the ANCOP guys were in formation. Their lateness was a letdown after the last training.

"I am all about having a nice sweat session before we start," Matt said, disgusted with the Afghans' failure to show up on time. "We're going to see a lot of boo-boo lips."

While they waited for the ANCOP to arrive, Matt explained what they were going to teach them. Instead of pursuing Taliban fighters, if the ANCOP got attacked, they were going to consolidate, return fire, and call for help. What the team didn't want was the ANCOP trying to chase down the fighters.

"They'll find themselves in downtown Zhari wearing the wrong uniform," Matt said. "Simplicity is the key here."

The training was going to start out slow. The idea was to get the ANCOP to crawl, then walk, and finally run. But that could only happen if the Afghans showed up to train in the first place.

Finally, Gregg got fed up with waiting. He marched off toward the barracks to round them up.

"It is fucking disrespectful," said Mike the Cop, shaking his head.

When Gregg got to the door of the barracks, ANCOP soldiers were piling out, pulling on uniform shirts and grabbing gear as they did so. He saw one of the officers and confronted him.

"Good morning, sir," Gregg said as Rza interpreted. "How come these guys aren't out front?"

The officer quickly spoke to Rza while Gregg waited for the translation.

"He said they are telling them to get their asses out here," Rza said.

As a former commando, Rza was having trouble hiding his contempt for the ANCOP. Later, during the drill, Gregg pointed out that one of the soldiers was not rotating in with the groups.

"Don't worry. He will die anyway," Rza said in a dismissive tone.

I'd seen Rza berate the policemen in the past. He mocked them and chastised them for not realizing the wealth of knowledge they had here at their fingertips. Rza considered the Special Forces his brothers because they had trained him to be a commando.

"If you have to go in there and kick their ass, that is what you do," Gregg told the officer through Rza.

Soon, about 30 of the more than 190 ANCOP cops at the base were gathered in a loose formation. Standing in two lines, they looked upset and were sulking, avoiding eye contact with Gregg.

"I just got off mission," said one ANCOP, who wore sunglasses and a Kevlar helmet. "I am sick and have a sore throat."

The comment set Gregg off.

"I don't want to hear a bunch of bullshit from you. I just got off mission too, a mission where we got shot at. But I am here. This shit is serious," Gregg barked at the formation. Rza translated, no doubt maintaining Gregg's angry tone. The ANCOP soldiers looked down at their feet.

Matt and the other team members watched Gregg.

"We can sweat it out of them," said Jeremy, ready to force the ANCOP to run and do push-ups and flutter kicks in the dust near their barracks.

Do they run them or do they leave? The team considered leaving for the day, but teaching the ANCOP to react under fire was too important.

"I say we smoke their balls. We're here to train them to save their lives," Jeremy said.

Gregg, firmly in the role of bad cop now, walked back over to the ANCOP formation. Taking up position in front of the men, Gregg, with Rza in tow, started in on them again. He wanted to impress upon them the importance of training because in a few short days they could be faced for real with the situation they were being trained in.

"You guys understand why we are doing this training. So you don't fucking die. We don't like coming out here sweating and crawling in the dirt," Gregg said. "But if you don't do it, you'll fucking die. If you don't want to take this seriously and get your asses out of bed, fuck it. I know how to do this. I am going to Zhari to kill motherfuckers. I am going to be fine."

Gregg paused to let Rza translate. The words seemed to hit the ANCOP like body blows. The Afghans were embarrassed now for not being ready to train. The team found out later that they were upset because their officer had been out the night before inspecting the checkpoints and had caught some of them sleeping. He'd yelled at the sleeping soldiers and now they had hurt feelings.

"I've worked with you for two months. I know you have families just like I do. I want you to see your families," Gregg continued. "That is why I am here. That is why these guys are here. Do us the respect of showing up on time and take this shit seriously."

When Gregg was done, "the Russian," an Afghan officer who looked more Western than his brethren, lectured the men about duty and being accountable. When he was done, Matt came over to continue the exercises. But he had to stop because some of the ANCOP, more angry than ashamed, had started to yell at the Russian, an ANCOP major.

"A couple of things. One, what the fuck is going on?" Matt said. "I have never seen so much disrespect for an officer. He is a major, man."

One of the ANCOP tried to plead his case, but Matt cut him off.

"Hey, shut up," he barked. "I don't give a fuck. It's not the time to talk back."

The Afghan stopped talking, but kept staring at Matt angrily.

"If I talked to an officer like that, I'd get punched in the fucking mouth. At the end of the day, you have to respect that they are an officer. If they come down on you hard, big deal, bro. You're a grown-up," Matt said. "You guys are good soldiers. You have to have thick skin. It happens. Just deal with it, bro. You're going to be all right. You're still breathing. Show some respect to your officers. They deserve it."

With the speech making over, Matt led the Afghans through the exercise. They set up a mock checkpoint using two green Afghan police trucks and split the trainees into two fifteen-man groups. Each group went through the exercise. Matt stood at one end of the road and started to make machine-gun noises as the Afghans bounded back—in buddy rushes—to the trucks, formed up on a line, and returned fire.

Each group was drilled on what to do. They practiced getting attacked from the front, rear, left, and right. When a soldier didn't remember what he was supposed to do in a specific situation, he had to run laps. As they went from crawling to walking to finally running, Matt or another team member would throw a flash-bang grenade to signify an attack.

"Get everybody down and shooting. Kill those bad guys," Matt said. "It is important for you to move fast, get down, and shoot back. They are going to have better fighting positions. The only way you're going to win is to get everybody to shoot back."

Matt constantly quizzed the trainees on what it was a checkpoint commander's job to do; they needed to know this in case they found themselves in a combat situation in which their commander was hit. Most of the soldiers knew what the commander would do: he'd tell them to fall back to the trucks and get on a line; then he would point out the direction, distance, and number of attackers; and finally he would call for reinforcements, for what was called a Quick Reaction Force or QRF. Matt drilled the Afghans over and over until they finally knew the procedures by heart.

He then took both groups on a short run that ended with him racing the whole group back to the checkpoint. Gathering them up afterward, Matt noticed one of the ANCOP balancing his gun on his foot.

"Get your weapon off your foot," he said, parting the group and snatching the rifle away from the Afghan.

"Carry your weapon like this," he continued, holding the rifle in both hands, the barrel pointed down toward the road.

Weapon safety is a huge issue with the soldiers and most treat their weapons like accessories. Their Chinese-made AK-47s were covered in dust and carried with no apparent concern for where the barrel was facing. Besides teaching the ANCOP how to set up checking points and survive under fire, the team was trying to instill a little professionalism.

"If it is not slung, you're holding it with both hands. *That* is professional," Matt said; weapons sergeant that he was, rifles, pistols, and machine guns were the tools of his trade. "Holding it in one hand. That is Taliban shit. Next guy I see holding it like that is running, bro."

Before he dismissed them, he reminded the Afghans that training started the following day at 9 A.M.

"I don't want to hear that your officer didn't tell you or my officer called me a shitbag," Matt said.

Back at the van, he thanked his teammates for coming out to help. He liked the way Gregg had played bad cop, and stressed the fact that he only wanted one guy a day being the bad guy and that the rest of the team was there to help train.

But tomorrow, if no one was outside waiting at nine o'clock, he was leaving.

"I am the QRF, bro," Matt said. "They are the guys that will get killed first."

CHAPTER 12

BUILDING BOHLE

A few days before the team permanently moved out to Wilson, I moved there with the team's support guys.

Ben, Mike the Cop, Littlejohn—the team's cook—and Day, who worked on the team's communications gear, moved with me. At this point, I'd essentially become a support guy too. I no longer got strange looks when I helped. Now it was expected, which was why the team sent me out early. The idea was for us to help Rick and Mike, the team's senior engineer, frame the rest of the containers and build the operations center.

After putting our gear in the transient tents, which sat down the road from the camp, we returned to find Mike the Cop moving his gear into his room. He'd selected a prefab green Afghan police checkpoint. It was essentially a container with paneled walls and a window and door cut out of one side. Built as a makeshift office, it had been acquired for the camp. And since Mike the Cop was a policeman at home, it was a no-brainer that he'd be the one who should live in it.

After the team left to go back to Kandahar, I sat outside in front of Mike's and Rick's rooms and they told me about the first days at the camp. Called Camp Bohle, it sat on the outer edge of Camp Wilson.

Special Forces soldiers name all their camps and buildings after soldiers who have been killed. The team had planned to name their new firebase Camp Mills, after another 7th Special Forces Group soldier, but they found out that the name was already slated for another camp.

"So, who is going to go out and get shot?" Matt joked.

They selected Camp Bohle next, naming their base after Sergeant First Class Bradley Scott Bohle. A medical sergeant assigned to the 3rd Battalion, 7th Special Forces Group, he was on his second deployment to Afghanistan when his truck was hit by an IED in Helmand Province in 2009. He died from the injuries.

When Rick and Mike first saw the site for Camp Bohle, it was a vast wasteland. A small Afghan compound, its walls crumbling from neglect, sat in the middle of the site. Nearby, squatters lived in a tent. They drove the water and fuel trucks that kept Camp Wilson going.

"Are you fucking kidding me?" Mike remembered saying, a look of disgust and contempt on his face. "Fuck, man, this is going to take forever."

For a few weeks before this, RC South—the regional command in charge of Coalition forces in southern Afghanistan—had been getting reports that the camp was ready. But after Rick and Mike finally had a look at the site, it was obvious that Camp Bohle was far from ready.

The work hadn't even begun.

After seeing the site, Rick and Mike knew they had to come out and get the camp going or when the team eventually got sent to the district they'd have nowhere to live. A few days later, Rick and Mike flew back out to Wilson and started building the camp. The first couple of days, they figured out whom they needed to talk to about obtaining supplies and mapped out a game plan.

They knew that they had to play the game, but at the same time they also knew that the system had already failed them and they would need to get things done their own way. Money to build the ANCOP's camp had been allocated, but no one had set aside funding for the Special Forces camp.

They considered just setting up tents, but ultimately that idea was nixed. Why use a tent when you know that you're going to have to live in a place for years? They decided on hard structures—a wooden operations center and containers converted into individual rooms.

Mike wanted to leave the camp in better condition than when he found it. He and Rick moved the squatters off, laid gravel, and found a bunch of containers that they set up in a loose U-shape. A welder cut out doorways and they started framing the inside with wooden walls and doors.

The next morning we started on the framing. I'm a terrible carpenter, but after some trial and error Mike the Cop and I got things working. We came up with a system for cutting the walls and ceiling boards and made steady progress framing Manny's room. Then Matt's. Then Josh's.

Since Manny had left Afghanistan because of a family emergency, Ben and I were told we could stay in his room. The work was slow. But there is something to building your own home. Essentially, I wasn't going to have a room unless I built it. Only Rick's and Mike's rooms were hooked up with power and the operations center had walls but no roof or power.

Even when the team finally arrived, the camp was still far from ready. And the ANCOP camp was worse. The tents were up, but they lacked both power and water. After arriving, Courtney and Colonel Agha went up to the headquarters to see about procuring some more tents to use until the camp was finished. A major from the 101st suggested that the ANCOP could just take showers using water bottles. That is when the captain's anger turned to rage.

"We don't treat our indig"—i.e. indigenous population—"that way," Courtney said later.

The ANCOP were supposed to stay at the Afghan National Army's camp, but the tents in which the police were supposed to live had been trashed and the Afghan Army soldiers put up wire separating them from the Army camp.

While a dirt road separated the Special Forces camp from the rest of Wilson, the rift between the soldiers was far bigger. One of the reasons Special Forces was so good at training foreign soldiers was that they treated them the same way as they would a U.S. unit. This created a bond that was hard to replace.

When Courtney saw the wire, he refused to let the ANCOP stay there. Instead, the Afghans took over the tents near the Special Forces camp, which were without power and water. That night, Courtney brought the team together. It was dark and hard to see, but you could tell by his voice and rigid body language that he was upset. He told the team that if they got into any trouble with the 101st or any other conventional units at Camp Wilson to refer the units to him or Tony.

"Be respectful. Tell them to talk with your team sergeant or captain," he said. "And I can tell them to pound sand, in a respectful way, so that they can read between the lines."

The next morning Courtney and Colonel Agha went up to meet Major Neumeyer, who was in charge of maintaining Camp Wilson. The colonel and Courtney sat across from Neumeyer, who sat behind his desk, a blank pad in front of him.

"There is a lot of work here to be done and your unit has a great reputation," the major said. "I know power is your number one concern. What are your other concerns for the camp?"

The list was long. Power. Water. Showers. Chow. But the colonel held his tongue.

"It is very impolite to complain about it," Agha said.

"My job is for people to be impolite to me," Neumeyer said.

Agha finally relented and said the camp needed power and water as soon as possible. The colonel said his men needed showers because of both sanitary and religious reasons.

"When you have a 'sweet dream' at night, it is customary to take a shower the next morning," the colonel said.

He said the prefab kitchen was useless without power, so he'd need access to the dining facility, and the ANCOP's trucks were also out of fuel. The Ministry of Interior hadn't provided them with supplies or fuel to continue their mission.

"We are prepared to do the mission, but we only have enough fuel to get to Zhari," the colonel said.

Neumeyer scribbled notes and seemed determined to fix the problems. He told the captain to allow the Afghan trucks access to the fuel point used by the American trucks and he'd get the dining hall to provide the ANCOP meals. By the end of the meeting, his once-blank pad was full of notes.

Back at Bohle, the rest of the team was working on getting their rooms and the operations center built. They knew the faster they got the camp up and running, the faster they'd be out doing missions.

When Tony started delegating jobs, my name was on the list. No longer was I there to observe. I'd become another attachment. Someone who had a primary job. Mine was to write a book, but my secondary job was to help the team. And that basically meant helping with everything from holding sheets of wood while Courtney and Tony nailed them into the crossbeams of the operations center to helping to "acquire" tin for its roof.

It was after dinner and the sun had already set. I was with Mike and Tony. They were working on getting Jake and Apollo a ride on a convoy back to Kandahar when they saw a pile of tin sheets lying next to the road.

"If they're there when we come back, I'm snagging them," Mike said.

On the ride back, the tin was still there. Pulling the truck up next to it, we hopped out and started throwing the sheets into the back. At first, we tried to pick up the whole stack, but it was too heavy. So, in pairs, we tossed the more than twenty sheets into the truck. Once, a truck came down the road, forcing us to hide. As soon as the headlights faded down the road, we were back to placing the sheets into the truck.

The whole thing was weird because while there was a degree of high school mischief to what we were doing, at the end of the day, these were supplies the team needed and just wasn't getting for whatever reason. Sometimes the end justifies the means. Even if it means reappropriating supplies that had not been earmarked for our use.

With all the sheets in the truck, Mike grabbed the wood pallet put in place to keep the tin off the ground.

"No evidence," Mike said.

When we got back to the camp, Courtney and Rick were out in front of the operations center. They had big smiles when Mike showed them what he'd acquired. The rest of construction went the same way. Mike was always scouring Wilson for more supplies or furnishings, including claiming what others didn't want.

Once, at the front gate, Mike found out that two latrines had arrived and no one claimed them.

"They're ours," he said to the driver. "When can you deliver them?"

Soon an Afghan crane operator dropped them down on one edge of the camp's U-shaped setup.

The containers had three showers and three toilets, the Eastern not Western version. At a glance, the toilet was just a hole in the floor with a small, raised six-inch-wide pad to put your feet on. There was no seat.

When the bathrooms arrived, Mike was the first inside to inspect the find. Poking his head into the stalls, he laughed.

"These are squatting shitters."

To use them, you had to squat like a baseball catcher over the hole. I'd used this kind of bathroom in the past in both Iraq and Afghanistan and had become pretty good at not crapping in my pants by accident. That was a real rookie mistake, and it happened. Guys would squat down and the turd would drop into their pants, which were bunched up around their ankles, instead of the hole.

Grabbing the white nozzle connected to a long hose—imagine a sprayer used to wash dishes—Mike waved it around.

"And they even have a bidet."

Before long, gray portable toilets that Gregg managed to acquire from some other medics were set up over the holes. Seems the team before had purchased the toilets to use in the field. But they worked perfectly in the new latrine.

The bathrooms were the last big addition. With power, air-conditioned rooms, and an operations center in which to plan, the camp was starting to feel like home.

And that meant the team was going to finally get into the fight.

CHAPTER 13

THE GUNS OF WILSON

The body-chattering boom of 105mm howitzers was the sound track of Camp Wilson.

At all hours of the night, and the day, the guns would be blasting away, sending rounds at targets far off in the district. At first, I chalked this up to the sounds of war. And assumed they were welcome sounds to the soldiers in combat. We had no idea where the rounds were landing or if they were actually bailing out soldiers in trouble. The guns were one of the chief protectors for the infantry troops who were crawling through the irrigation canals or crossing the fields looking for Taliban fighters.

In some ways it felt good to be close to the war or at least what seemed like a battle. But that feeling lasted only about a day. The booms quickly started to grate on my nerves.

Inside the containers, the shock wave that accompanied each boom vibrated through the metal walls, rattling the wooden frame of the structure, and echoing for a few seconds. Outside, you could hear a crackling sound as the shell broke the sound barrier overhead. Sometimes, the rounds hit and exploded. But often the shells exploded in the air, releasing a flare that lit up the area and then dissipated into a wisp of smoke.

The first time I heard them shoot overhead, I jumped up out of bed. The shock wave flung open the door to the room and rattled the ceiling so much that I thought it was going to fall in on top of me. Six more shots in succession shook the container enough to give me a headache. It took more than a week before I stopped jumping. But after a while, the booms faded into the background noise. The only times I noticed was when I talked on the phone with my family at home.

Once, I was talking to my brother before his next football game when the guns started throwing rounds downrange. I paused to wait for the boom to fade.

"What was that? You getting attacked?" he asked.

"Those are just the guns," I replied. But immediately I felt stupid. Thousands of miles away in Raleigh, North Carolina, the guns sounded dangerous, but for me it was just another day at Wilson.

The constant artillery was driving Jake's dog, Apollo, crazy. Each round would send the once-fierce German shepherd scurrying into Jake's room or bounding out of the room looking for him if he wasn't there. It became so bad that Jake had to get the dog out of the camp. But losing Jake and Apollo bothered Gregg; he saw the loss of the dog as the team losing one of its primary means of detecting IEDs.

So, a few weeks after our arrival, Jake was gone. But not before he built a pair of wooden steps with carpentry skills that would have made Jesus Himself envious.

During one team meeting, Gregg asked what the captain planned to do about the IED threat.

"That is the only way they can get us," he said.

Everybody in the room knew that he was right, and the prospect of going out on missions without a means of finding the bombs was unnerving. But the team had no choice. Apollo had to go and it would be weeks before the team could procure another dog.

The reality didn't sit well with Gregg and only cemented his reputation as a guy with an attitude problem.

"Once I got into the Army, I decided that sugarcoating things wasn't necessarily the way to go," Gregg commented later. "I just thought that to not effectively convey your points, or your concerns, because you're worried about bruising someone's ego, can mean death or dismemberment to a friend."

But that really didn't explain it all. I'd spent a lot of time with Gregg and really believed that he wasn't one to go along with things without thinking about them first. In some ways, it was one of the reasons why the Army chose him to be part of an elite community, but on the flip side he never got comfortable with the Army's being, in his eyes, a big bureaucratic pig that lumbered at its own pace for its own reasons.

As an X-Ray, Gregg hadn't fully embraced life in the Army. Instead, he tried to straddle the line between compliance and rebellion. He was quick to chaff at "stupid Army stuff." He questioned everything and never had enough patience for the "it is what it is" response; he couldn't just go along with the Army's way. Gregg argued that even though he was new to the Army, his life experience exceeded most of the other guys', except for Manny and Rick.

"Team leadership seems to foster a go-along-with-the-flow type of success recipe," Gregg said. "To raise a voice is to have an attitude problem."

Life on the camp was starting to fall into a pattern. Matt started the P90X exercise program and worked out in the mornings, often pushing himself until he threw up. He'd run in the evenings. I made the mistake of running with him once and stayed with him for about fifty yards before he dusted me. I spent the rest of the run trying to keep him in sight. Josh, Gregg, Jeremy, and the others started to go to the gym near the dining hall.

With the routine of a working camp in place, Courtney, Rick, and Tony started planning missions. The first step was to figure out when the checkpoints would be ready. They also wanted to start meeting with the other units in the 101st brigade's area to get a sense of what was going on in the district.

Courtney let me tag along at one of the meetings. Riding up in one of the trucks the team used to get around the camp, we parked outside one of the unit's operations center, a plywood building near Wilson's airfield. The unit owned the eastern part of Zhari and two of the proposed ANCOP checkpoints were in their area.

Courtney knocked on the door and was greeted by a young specialist. Seeing us, the specialist turned back to talk with an officer.

"Hey, sir, there are some contractors here," he called over his shoulder.

We all looked at one another and chuckled. But Courtney and Tony seemed annoyed by the comment.

Seeing the men dressed in civilian clothes, dirty from the sawdust, the specialist, I guess, had made an honest mistake. At this point, my sparse beard had grown into a tangle of brown, red, and far more gray than I'd anticipated. Since I'd been seen with the team from the start, no one questioned who I was or what I was doing. So, I'd go to meetings like this one and take a seat at the table. Often, the officers we'd visit would make eye contact with me during the brief like I was a somebody. I, of course, benefited from the association of Special Forces and the aura that they radiated. For all I knew, the conventional officers thought I was some civilian spook or specialist attached to the team.

A few minutes after the specialist finally invited us in, a bleary-eyed major walked up to us. He looked haggard with puffy red eyes. Holding a packet of PowerPoint slides, he ordered someone in the operations center to get the package ready to brief and then guided us back to his office. This operations center was laid out like all the others I had seen. Men were huddled over computers. A large screen dominated the main wall. On it were Predator feeds and footage taken from the large white blimp that hovered over the camp. It was the blimp that the commanders used to track the small groups of insurgents as they moved from compound to compound in the district. It was Big Brother's never-blinking eye in the sky.

As the team gathered around a map of the area in his office, I noticed that the major had put his blue cavalry hat on a stand in the corner. It was pristine with a sparkling gold cord. Like the cavalry of old, he was chasing Indians, but this time with high-tech sensors and guns that could reach all the way down the valley. The problem, though, was the lack of ground being taken. The unit failed to hold anything except for a few outposts and spent most of its time keeping the Indians off their doorstep.

Courtney told me on the ride up that in five months, the 101st had cleared no more than seven hundred meters south of the highway. American troops patrolled the area, but they knew very little about the human terrain.

During the briefing, the major never once mentioned any of the village elders or gave any detail about who or what was in the village. All he did was offer a tour of fire missions, including a recent one in which he shot several smoke rounds into a field. As soon as the rounds hit, he saw a dozen men jump up and run to a compound. Since none of the men had a gun, he couldn't shoot at them.

I had a feeling that had I been talking to 101s soldiers on the ground this might have been different. The only thing operations centers do is control and deconflict missions. They digest piles of reports, but really the only guys who understand it are the guys leaving the base on a daily basis.

The one time the major did point to a village, all he said was "this cluster fuck here is Zendanan. This is your problem child." He then pointed to a nearby canal that fighters used to move around in under cover. His men took fire near it, so they hit it with several rounds. When the soldiers returned and tried to do a damage assessment, basically a look to see if they'd hit anything, any wounded or dead fighters had been removed.

"Somebody is calling the shots. There had been a solid withdrawal," the major said. "The cas evac"—the evacuation of casualties—"was lightning fast."

The unit's fire missions were essentially nothing more than chasing the insurgents around the battlefield. Like shooting at a fly in your room with a handgun. All they accomplished was maybe kill a few fighters, if the soldiers were lucky, but they failed to hold ground or build any rapport with the locals.

But in the last few days, the major said, the fighters had been disorganized and were not being reinforced.

"Sustained attacks are few and far between," he told us.

On the ride back, Courtney, Rick, and Tony let it be known that they weren't impressed with the situation. It appeared that little progress was being made. And there was no link, no rapport, between the people and the 101st soldiers, which, as I've said before, was a key part of the counterinsurgency strategy. This fact was a source of much frustration to the captain, and it was one of the first things he and his team were going to try to remedy by getting out and talking to people.

Was the situation too dangerous? Was the threat the insurgents posed so high that it would be impossible to make any meaningful connection with the locals?

Before he became an ODA commander, Courtney was a platoon leader. The biggest difference between the two positions had to do with the way he had to approach a mission.

As a platoon leader, he had always questioned things that didn't make sense to him, once asking why his company in the 10th Mountain Division always went out in Humvees when the Taliban had spotters around the base watching the company move. The mission then under discussion had to do with setting up ambushes along rat lines, and he asked the battalion commander if they could use other vehicles or another way to transport the troops out so the spotters didn't see them.

His battalion commander told him he was too unconventional, which shouldn't be a surprise since Courtney was focused on being in Special Forces since his days at the Citadel, a military college in South Carolina.

The captain had excelled in junior ROTC during high school in Washington and his teachers pushed him to apply for admission to a service academy or military school. He always had a thing for being in the military. His father died when he was nine years old, and his mother told him that his father had wanted him to go to a military school.

The captain chose the Citadel in Charleston, South Carolina, over other military schools. He wanted to go to medical school and joined the Air Force ROTC when he enrolled, but the Air Force didn't have any scholarships his freshman year. So he transferred to the Army, got a scholarship, and soon fell in with a group of students targeted for special operations.

Many of Courtney's mentors were Green Berets, and they took

him under their wing. He participated in the Ranger Challenge—a grueling skills competition—three years in a row, and after completing advance training at Fort Lewis, he spent two weeks in the woods playing a guerrilla in Pineland, the fictional country in North Carolina where all Special Forces soldiers complete "Robin Sage," the course's final exam.

Now hooked on Special Forces, Courtney abandoned his medical school dreams and made infantry his first choice. Combat engineer and military police were his second and third. All of his unit preferences were light infantry. He wanted the 82nd Airborne Division first, followed by the 101st Airborne, and finally the 10th Mountain Division.

He was selected for the infantry, but was sent to the 10th Mountain. After graduation, he completed Ranger school and was sent to the 2nd Battalion, 87th Infantry Regiment. The unit was deployed to Afghanistan, so less than a month after he signed into the unit he was on a plane to Afghanistan.

He was sent to a company in the Bermel district of the country, a region his battalion commander called the "Wild Wild West." The area is very remote, and runs along the border with Pakistan. When he took over his platoon, his men were shocked to learn that he was only twenty-two years old, so much so that they demanded to see his driver's license.

But the platoon members didn't have time to dwell on his youth and inexperience because the following day the unit rolled out on a combat mission and Courtney's first firefight. It shocked him at first to hear the bullets pinging off his truck. But the radio crackled to life instantly. It was his platoon sergeant.

"Hey sir, what do you want us to do?"

He felt at first that he was the one who should be asking this question, but from that moment on, he didn't think. He just led.

"I want you to lay down suppressing fire," he told me he replied, during some downtime we shared a few days later. "And I need the direction and distance so that I can call it up."

Courtney said that some of the best men he'd served with had been members of that platoon, but he had an eye toward selection. So, when he got home, he became Brigadier General Jeffrey Buchanan's aide and started training for selection. He'd work out twice a day, once in the morning and once in the afternoon. The general, an ultra-marathon runner, helped him set up his cardio training plan. He followed the plan for five months.

When Courtney got to Fort Bragg for selection in June 2008, he was ready. The possibility of failure never crossed his mind.

"At the end of the day, it comes down to heart and drive," he told me.

The big push in the officer portion of the Q course has to do with thinking unconventionally.

"As long as you understand what is inside the box, thinking outside is easy," the captain said.

The captain was confident that he could change the way the war was going in the district by staying outside the box. He had a battalion of cops that could go anywhere in the district. And he had the will to start making the necessary connections with the people. Because if there was one thing that was for sure, it was that the current Whac-A-Mole strategy wasn't working.

CHAPTER 14

BATTLEFRONT

Just after breakfast, I arrived at the camp only to see some of the team standing on the containers we used as rooms and the ten-foot-tall concrete walls surrounding the camp. Overhead, a pair of OH-58 Kiowa Warrior helicopters and a lone AH-64 Apache circled a tree line less than a kilometer from the highway.

I crawled up on top of one of the trucks with Mike the Cop and we watched as the helicopters took turns diving at the trees and letting loose with bursts of machine-gun fire. Each strafing run sounded like a long zipper being undone. There was a poof of white smoke followed by the faint thud of the rounds hitting.

The Apache, slower than the smaller Kiowa scout helicopters, raked the trees several times before finally firing a hellfire. The rocket sent up a cloud of dust that hung over the tree line for several minutes. The Kiowas—with their distinct observation globe over the rotors— followed with several barrages of rockets that also hit the tree line.

Between attacks, the helicopters raced around the camp in

one long circle before swooping in like angry insects to sting the tree line with rounds and rockets. Later, an A-10 arrived overhead. As the helicopters cleared away on another circuit around the camp, the fighter slid out of the sky like a hawk and let loose thousands of rounds from its 30mm cannon before pulling up and gently rolling over in the crystal-blue sky.

From the camp, it was a live-fire air show. A show of force that was almost scary. It was amazing to watch the lethal firepower that the U.S. forces were able to bring from the air. It was almost as if God Himself reached down from the clouds and smashed the tree line.

For those of us who witnessed it, it was a welcome reminder that all that hammer swinging we'd had to do in order to build the camp was just a means to an end. We'd soon be out there confronting whatever the helicopters were now pummeling.

As we watched, Mike made a good point. The center of gravity, the war's main effort, was less than a kilometer from the gate. A few days before, General David Petraeus, the commander of all forces in Afghanistan, told the 101st that the division's 2nd Brigade at Wilson was the "main effort of the world," or MEOW. The acronym made its way onto a sign, hung on the door of the planning shop, showing a cat holding a mini–sniper rifle.

Kandahar had become a decisive battlefield. A place that the United States and, according to intelligence reports, Taliban leader Mullah Omar had chosen to finish this war. And the fight in Zhari would mark the next phase in the plan.

"There is no better place to be," Mike the Cop declared. Despite all the jerking around and the start-and-stop missions in Kandahar City, the team finally had a chance to get moving and play a role in what could be the biggest operations of the war.

The Zhari district had been created from territories taken from the Maywand and Panjwai districts. With a population estimated at more than eighty thousand, it was located on the north bank of the Arghandab River, just a few miles from Wilson; thus it was sometimes called the Arghandab Valley. It was there that Mullah Omar founded the Taliban when he hanged a warlord from the turret of a tank after the warlord raped two teenagers in 1994.

Members of the Quetta Shura, composed of the Taliban's top leaders running the war from the safety of Pakistan, owned the district's land. It was through here that fighters funneled weapons, drugs, and bomb-making supplies to Kandahar.

After the battle, I went down to the operations center to talk with Tron. I wanted to get a better handle on what to expect since a patrol was planned for the following day. Tron told me that Taliban leaders had met in Pakistan to discuss the battle plan for post-Eid operations. They came up with the following guidance:

1. Holding ground in the rural parts of Kandahar Province is the objective. Do not start an offensive, just sit and wait out Coalition forces because they won't stay. When Coalition forces come in, either leave or hide and wait.

2. Focus attacks on urban areas in Kandahar City. Use rapid surprise suicide attacks followed by ambushes. Keep Coalition forces in their bases and not out helping the people. The idea is to persuade the people that the Coalition is not here to help, but to stay in their bases and destroy Afghanistan.

3. Do not engage in sustained attacks with Afghan or Coalition forces. Hit-and-run attacks only.

Tron said he and Courtney talked about using the ANCOP to build up security around the base and checkpoints.

"The idea is to create security bubbles that get bigger as the population buys in," Tron said. "We can still affect the population. We are really putting an Afghan face on the battlefield. It is the best mission because we are doing a bit of everything."

This was Tron's fourth time in Afghanistan. During his first two tours he was with a team in the eastern provinces along the Pakistani border. In 2009, he came with the battalion headquarters and hated it.

Tron said things had changed for Special Forces since the early part of the war. The rules were more restrictive and conventional units now had more say over what they did. In the past, the teams could operate at will, oftentimes without the conventional units in the area having any idea of what they were doing.

Moreover, the teams had lived in remote firebases and had been told to disrupt the enemy. Once they did this, it was up to them to map the human terrain, figure out who the bad guys were, set up an intelligence network, and kill the bad guys.

He said that this was what the team had done in Khost, done with a lot of success. Forward Operating Base Salerno, the massive conventional base in the area, was known as Rocket City because of the number of rockets that hit the base. But when Tron's team started working in the area, the number of rockets shot at the base dwindled because the team knew who were the main players and had contacts that would lead them to suppliers and shooters.

The same kind of thing was needed in Zhari. The team needed to "learn the people" because the farther south the 101st pushed, the more dangerous it was going to get as the fighters found themselves squeezed between Zhari and Panjwai, another area where the Taliban leaders owned land and that they called home.

Nevertheless he didn't expect much of a fight.

Intelligence reports said that the Quetta Shura was short on money, and with winter coming, most of its members lacked the will to fight hard. Instead, they'd likely regroup and wait for the spring and the next year's poppy crop to fill their wallets.

"The TB will leave when they see the ANCOP because the Afghan police, unlike the Coalition, will be a constant presence," Tron said. "They are going to stay and watch and see what we do. They are going to watch and see how the population reacts."

The next day, the team finally went on a mission. For Rick and Mike, it was the first time they'd been "outside the wire" in any meaningful manner. The team was going to the 2nd Battalion, 502nd Infantry Regiment's headquarters to talk about checkpoints. The unit was located at a smaller base west of Wilson on the same highway.

As the convoy slowly rolled out of Wilson, I could feel a little tension. This wasn't the same old shit in Kandahar City. This was a new area. A real battleground.

Standing in the back of the RG next to Tron, I watched the farmland slip by. As I scanned to the south, it was impossible not to think about the insurgent fighters moving down in that area. Especially after all of the fireworks we'd seen over the last few days.

Tron, wearing a skull dust mask, waved to the kids on the side of the road as they watched the convoy go by. All of the kids waved back. The farmers were another story. Few of them waved back or even looked up as the convoy passed.

When we got to the base, the convoy pulled along the side of the road as Courtney went up to the front gate.

Rick jumped out with Rza and stood on the highway. The ANCOP and ANA tried to keep traffic moving. It was dangerous to be stopped on the road. It made you an easy target for a suicide bomber. Suddenly a beat-up silver compact car raced out of a pack of cars. Rza and some of the ANCOP threw up their hands. The driver quickly slammed on his brakes when he saw the ANCOP.

The car stopped right in front of Rza and Rick.

Standing in the back of the truck, I could see the driver hunkered down. His head was covered in a scarf. White smoke billowed from the back of the car as it skidded to a halt in front of the base. Rick, raising his rifle, started to back up slowly. The car and driver fit the suicide-bomber profile. White turban. White robe. Wide eyes and a crazed look on his face.

Rza clearly had the same thought as he shouted at the driver in Pashto to move. Everything was happening so quickly that I didn't have a chance to hunker down in the truck. It felt like I was moving in water. I knew this could be trouble, but I couldn't get my body to find cover. I was just waiting for the fireball.

Rza shouted for the driver to move then fired a single shot from his AK-47 into the pavement near the car's rear tire. With the driver now hunkered down so low in the seat that it was difficult to see his head, the car suddenly skidded away. The engine screamed as he rammed the pedal down, leaving a stream of white smoke in his wake.

Rick and Rza retreated back toward the trucks. Rick had a grin on his face as he walked by me.

"Fuck. I thought, 'That guy is going to kill me,'" he said to Rza as the two passed. "For a split second, I was sure that was the end."

Pulling into the camp, I went with Rick, Tony, Courtney, and Agha to meet with Major White, the battalion's operations officer. Like the 101st officer at Wilson, he had a weary look in his eyes as he greeted the team at the tactical-operations-center door. Ushering us into a conference room, he went to get some maps.

"I didn't like the vibe already," Rick said after White left.

When White got back, he had a map and a packet of PowerPoint slides showing the location of the checkpoints. I noticed the puffy red rings under his eyes as he spread out the map.

"We don't have the checkpoints ready," he said almost apologetically. "I had a local-national contractor ready to build them. He got shot going back to Kandahar City."

You could see the energy deflate out of the team. Another setback. Another problem. Another promise unfulfilled. White went on to tell him that the earliest he could get a checkpoint up was in a few weeks. The checkpoints were supposed to stop Taliban fighters' movements and ambushes along Highway One.

But the delay created an opening. Not only for the Taliban but, as it turned out, for the team.

"Brigade is telling me that I've got to open up Route Langley and I need some combat power to do that," White said. "I've got no police out here. What I am proposing is that we take your part of the force and base you at Spin Pir with the ability to patrol the highway and bazaar."

The team's first break. Essentially, the 101st was trying to secure a road—named Route Langley—that ran north–south from the highway. They'd built two smaller outposts and wanted the team to take over one near a village along the route. Courtney jumped at the chance to flex the ANCOP's muscles and work them off the checkpoints and into the populace, where his team could focus on the people and finding a future Village Stability Operations (VSO) site.

On the flip side, the 101st increased the number of troops they had on their push to the south and left behind an Afghan force to hold the meager amount of real estate they'd cleared.

The whole time, Habib translated for Colonel Agha. With all the Americans in agreement, the decision finally went to the colonel.

But the Afghan wasn't buying it. Agha said his bosses in the Ministry of Interior wouldn't let the ANCOP stay in a base like Spin Pir or Pulchakhan—which was built next to the highway—without ANA or

American soldiers. He wanted to be assured that if the base was attacked, the Americans could help call in a Quick Reaction Force or close air support.

"Will you be staying there with us?" Agha asked the captain.

"Yeah," Courtney said. "We'll be there on almost a constant basis."

CHAPTER 15

ALMOST ACTION

Fran, the Canadian who supervised the security guards on this base, sped up to our camp and hopped out in a cloud of dust.

Fran said that enemy fighters had fired a recoilless rifle at their southern tower and he wanted Matt to bring up his sniper rifle and see if they could catch the Taliban fighters because the Tundra guards on the wall had seen their location. (Tundra is a private security company based in Toronto that sent contractors to Afghanistan.)

At a glance, Fran looked like the typical contractor. Thick beard. Thick chest. Tattoos, including a black band on his forearm with MOLON LABE written on it. The phrase is attributed to the Spartan King Leonidas, who said it before the Battle of Thermopylae. It loosely translates as "come and take them" and was said when the Persians asked the Spartans to lay down their arms. The phrase is also the motto of United States Special Operations Command Central, which oversees operations in the Middle East and Afghanistan.

Fran had been in Afghanistan with the Canadian Army a few years before, but had been making his living as a contractor for the last couple of years. He'd mastered FOB—Forward Operating Base—living and had a nice hooch with Internet, Indian cable TV, and air-conditioning. Plus, it was located on one of the quiet corners of the base. Ben and I went over on occasion to use his wireless Internet. Each time we went, the room was packed with guests. Mostly 101st soldiers seeking some respite from Army living.

Fran, Rick, and Mike had hit it off almost as soon as the team got to the base and Fran helped them get supplies for the base. By extension, Fran was a de facto member of the team. So, when he showed up with good intelligence, the team was eager to check it out.

Matt raced back to his room and grabbed a sniper rifle. A few nights before, we'd been talking about finally getting to see some action.

"It's been too long. I need a good gunfight," Matt said.

The team had spent the last week building the camp, and all the work had taken its toll. With the camp at last in working order, it was time to get into the fight. The whole team looked forward to getting out and patrolling. Even I was looking forward to getting some missions.

Matt and I were sitting outside of our rooms with Gregg and Ben. It was getting dark and soon we wouldn't be able to see one another, only our shadowy outlines and the sound of our voices. After a whole day of work, the nights often turned into marathon conversations. We'd all grab a chair and sit in front of Rick and Mike's room. Gregg, fresh from a shower, would usually spend ten minutes or so shirtless and in "Ranger panties"—the short black shorts favored by runners—while he smeared lotion all over his legs and chest. It was uncomfortable to watch him and only the darkness saved us from really getting a good look at his floor show. Sometimes these impromptu parties lasted a few hours, but most of the time we'd slowly peel away, returning to our separate rooms to watch movies or surf the Internet.

But on this night, Matt started talking about his first firefight a few years before.

He was in an alley between two compounds when a Taliban fighter fired an RPG at the door. He said everything suddenly seemed to slow down, and as the rocket-propelled grenade shot past him, he could see its rotation and the fin stabilizers spinning by.

"I could have reached out and grabbed it, bro," he said.

The rocket exploded farther down the alley. A teammate who was on the roof peeked down to make sure he was okay, but Matt had already started to fire back. He was with Afghan commandos and grabbed the one with the machine gun. Pointing toward the fighters, he told the Afghan to fire. Scared, the Afghan just held the gun out around the corner and sprayed.

"So I punched him in the mouth. Boom!" Matt said, miming the punch. "And I snatched the gun away."

Giving it to another commando, Matt continued to fire. As he told the story he became excited all over again. He seemed to feed off the energy of battle and craved the action.

Now, back at Camp Bohle with the Canadian contractor Fran, Rick and Matt jumped into Fran's Toyota Hilux (think Tacoma), and sped to the gate with Fran, followed by John, Ben with his camera, and Mike. I followed in another truck driven by Gregg.

Speeding around curves and obstacles, we finally got to the wall. We found everyone on the outer wall of the Tundra's camp. Mike, Matt, and Ben were lying on top of a tower overlooking the highway. Rick, behind a massive spotting scope, was a step below and scanning the green fields to the south of the camp.

They were tracking at least one person who looked to have been holding a rifle in the shade of a tree line, approximately half a mile away. He was near a car, which was a perfect getaway.

"Is that a car? Well, you see it, right?" Rick said.

"Yeah, I just don't know if that's a car or a truck," Mike said, looking through the sniper scope. "It's in the shade about halfway is what it looks like."

"There were two people," Rick said. "Just behind that thing."

Bruno, another Tundra guy and Fran's boss, was next to Rick with a set of binoculars. Both were glassing the valley. If they saw one rifle, they could shoot.

"Mike, you see where the sheep are at?" Rick yelled up as Mike dialed the scope in. Matt was lying nearby with his rifle trained on the valley.

"Yeah, that building?" Mike said, getting comfortable behind the stock of the rifle.

"Yeah, that building. It looks like a guy in the bushes."

Mike strained to see the man, but couldn't locate him. John took a look too with his M4 sight, but didn't see him.

After weeks of inaction, Mike was feeling an almost primal need to fire the sniper rifle. Weeks of just swinging a hammer had made it imperative that he once again use his combat skills. Silently, everyone on the wall just prayed that a weapon materialized so that they could start shooting.

Standing next to a contractor wearing a tan Boston Red Sox hat, I waited for a target or for the other guys to quit and pack up the rifle. Nearby, Gregg, wearing a Derek Jeter shirt, scanned the fields with his rifle.

"Derek Jeter sucks," the contractor said to Gregg.

Gregg smiled. Lowering his rifle, he looked back at the contractor.

"Yeah, and I'd like to congratulate your team for its great postseason," Gregg said.

The Red Sox had come in third in the American League East, behind the Devil Rays and the Yankees, that year. A sore spot for any Red Sox fan, including me. There really wasn't much to add. The Sox were out. The Yanks were in, and all I could do was cheer for the Rangers because I couldn't deal with another Yankees World Series.

I wasn't alone.

"I've got nothing to say," the contractor said.

Rick and Mike continued to scan for a target. Two Afghan kids on bikes pedaled down the highway. One bike had a siren that wailed. The kid hit it over and over as they passed.

Still no men. No rifle. Nothing.

Soon farmers started coming out from the nearby houses. All of the excitement was just daily life in southern Afghanistan for them. The crops needed to be tended and the field plowed even if a bunch of soldiers insisted on fighting a war around them.

But for Rick and the others, it was a missed shot. A chance to make shooting at the base a two-way street. The guys with the capes were there, but they couldn't hit back if they didn't have anything to hit.

Frustrated, we all returned to camp in silence because there really was nothing to say.

War was boring.

CHAPTER 16

OUR HONEY

Sitting on the floor of Colonel Agha's trailer, the Afghans were passing out paper plates of food.

The ANCOP officers had invited the captain, Rick, and Tony over to their camp for dinner. With the construction winding down, everybody knew we'd soon be running missions and the Afghans wanted to toast the occasion and strengthen the bond between the units.

It was Friday—the Afghans' only day off—and after a week of building we were all anxious to celebrate. It was also my first chance to really meet the Afghans. I'd been on a few missions with them in Kandahar City, but they'd been working and I had no time to really talk with them. Plus, we were from drastically different cultures, lived on separate camps, and didn't speak each other's language.

I'd spent more time with the interpreters—Habib, Rza, and Big Rza. Habib was by far the most ambitious of the three. I pegged him for a future warlord since he seemed to be so well connected—he was a name-dropper who liked to talk about all the commanders he knew—and bragged about dating some commander's daughter in Kabul.

Rza and Big Rza were former commandos. They were inseparable and had taken on the job of interpreters only as a means to stay in the fight. Both were Hazara, the Shiite Muslims who compose the third largest ethnic group of Afghanistan, both had wives waiting for them, and both wanted to go to the United States. Courtney was trying to help Rza complete his paperwork so that he could obtain a visa and move to San Diego.

Getting to know the translators was one thing, but trying to get below the surface with the ANCOP guys was more difficult. So, I took the Afghan's invitation to dinner in hopes of at least getting a sense of things in the other camp.

As we walked through their gate, the ANCOP officers met us at the door and made sure we had the most comfortable pillows to lounge against.

The camp still lacked electricity, and there were holes in the wall for the eventual power lines that would run the Chigo air conditioner and bring electricity to the plugs. In one corner sat the same TV that Namatullah watched in Kandahar. It was dark, without power. The windows of the trailer were open and a light breeze made things bearable. The officers kept the door open to keep the air circulating, but the room soon grew warm as all of us crowded inside.

Since the ANCOP ate out of the chow hall like us, the food they served was from the day's dinner menu. It was presented well; each of us got a plate of chicken nuggets, green beans, and rice. Small silver platters of sliced tomatoes and peppers were placed next to the plates, which added a little spice to the bland rice.

There was a real ceremonial feel to the whole dinner. I felt like a houseguest, and the Afghans, Agha's officers, were working to show me and the other guys the truest hospitality.

Courtney on patrol in southern Afghanistan.

Gregg shakes hands with two Afghan children during a patrol.

Unless otherwise noted, all photos by Ben Watson

Gregg takes a short break during a patrol.

Josh on the rear gun during a convoy in southern Afghanistan.

Kandahar City shot from a Black Hawk.
Courtesy of the author

The author on patrol with the team and ANCOP.

Mike the cop mans the rear gun during a convoy to Camp Bohle.
The hill in the background is on the outskirts of Kandahar City.

Rick takes a knee during a patrol near Camp Bohle.

Ben reads at Camp Bohle. The team's operations center is in the background.
Courtesy of the author

Matt and Habib talk to some kids in Kandahar's District 9.

Jeremy talks on the radio before a patrol. Notice the team patch on his right sleeve.

An ANCOP soldier patrols in southern Afghanistan.
Courtesy of the author

An Afghan boy carries a toy AK-47 in Kandahar City.
The guns were a hot Ramadan gift.

Close-up of a toy gun found on the streets of Kandahar in 2010.

An Afghan boy aims a toy gun at an American convoy in Kandahar City.

The author with an ANCOP soldier outside of Kandahar.
Notice the author's first-aid kit on the left side of his body armor.

Josh sports his mullet wig during election day.

Josh wearing his mullet wig while the team shoots on the range.

Matt fires at a zombie target.

The ANCOP train at their barracks near Kandahar.
The team spent a whole morning teaching the ANCOP how to survive an ambush.

The team works on the operations center at Camp Bohle.

The author and Matt throw a baseball at Camp Bohle.

The author and Gregg watch the ANCOP train for an upcoming patrol.

Josh, Matt, and Tron pose for a picture
before an early-morning patrol near Camp Bohle.

Rick fires a smoke grenade into a field during a patrol.
The team was hoping to draw Taliban fighters out.

Rza was one of the team's best interpreters.
A former commando, he walked and talked like a Green Beret.

Tron poses in front of a massive field of marijuana during a patrol near Camp Bohle.

The author before a patrol in southern Afghanistan.

about war, armies, and all the other notions glorified by warriors and writers who can afford to rhapsodize far from the battlefield.

"I trust you with my life," the colonel told the Americans.

"And at the end of the day, all we're going to have is each other out there," Courtney said back.

Soon, all of the Afghans started smoking. Rick and Ben also had a cigarette and within a short while a thick haze was hanging over the whole room. As bottle after bottle emerged from the box, all the serious talk gradually faded into jokes, which started with Rick's tattoos.

The designs completely covered his arms. He had crusader crosses and knights, symbols from his motorcycle club back in North Carolina. It was impossible not to notice them.

"You are like a bad person," Agha teased Rick, and laughed. "When I get back to Herāt, I'm going to get my own," he continued, miming the sleeves that he planned to get.

"We don't judge a book by its cover," was Rick's terse response.

Since it was his trailer, when Agha spoke everyone listened. The more the colonel drank, the more he dominated the conversation. When Rick or anyone else tried to talk, he cut them off.

"Break. Break."

Break was radio code for a pause when transmitting a message. Agha had the floor and he wanted to make sure the Americans understood the bond they'd forged with him and his men.

"We're brothers. Sometimes we're going to laugh," the colonel said. "Sometimes we're going to fight. But we're always brothers."

But what Colonel Agha really wanted to talk about was the soldier's mind. He asked the Americans to be patient with his men because, as he put it, sometimes a soldier was physically there but his mind was elsewhere. Like at home in Herāt or with his family in Kabul.

It was a strange kind of apology for the lapses in judgment we'd witnessed at Camp Wilson and for ANCOP's poor performance at the training session in Kandahar. It seemed to me that Agha was trying to clear the slate before he and the team went out into Zhari. He didn't want the team to think his men were undisciplined.

"The reason why Afghans don't listen . . ." Agha went on, "the reason they don't remember your advice is because they have a thousand thoughts going through their minds. All of the stuff that is troubling their lives."

Agha said his men worried about their families. They worried that their paycheck wasn't big enough. He said if a soldier's family called and told him they needed him home in two days or they needed money because someone was sick, he was going to be thinking about that instead of thinking about the mission.

"You might think they are undisciplined or are not listening, but we cannot blame them for that," the colonel concluded.

Rick agreed and told the colonel that his own guys had the same problems.

"We have problems at our houses. Just like your men, we are away from home," Rick said. "You're not alone here. If there is a problem, we can find a solution together."

Rick told Agha about his 2008 deployment. He was going through a divorce and it was weighing on his mind. He admitted that at times it was hard to keep all the different pieces separate and compartmentalized. But he did it, and when it was time to focus on the mission, that is what he did.

"We all have problems, but I had to do what I had to do," Rick said.

While the colonel kept waxing poetic about brotherhood and interrupting Rick, Tony was teaching the Afghans Spanish words and they taught him Dari words. Simple things like "plate," "fork," "peach," and "whiskey." Joker was his best pupil, but he kept putting his hand high on Tony's thigh. Every once in a while, Tony would push it away, but a few minutes later it would be back. When men hold hands in Afghanistan, it's a sign of friendship. But at the moment all the touching was obviously making Tony uncomfortable.

Out of all the Afghan officers, Joker was the weirdest.

Balding and short, he earned his nickname because he always had this creepy grin on his face. He was very "touchy" with his men and the Americans, when they got in range. I saw him several times and each time he wanted to shake my hand and give me an awkward half hug. Even though Joker was supposed to be engaged to be married, we were convinced he liked men more than women.

The rumors about Afghan homosexuality were rampant. The Americans call Thursday, the day before the Afghans' only day off, "man-love Thursday," and the following day "asshole-repair Friday." I heard several stories about guys catching Afghan soldiers giving each other hand jobs, or claiming to hear the most god-awful howling during Thursday nights.

Soon all eyes were on Tony when Agha learned that they'd missed his birthday. It had been few days before. We'd all been busy building the camp and only made passing mention of it. Tony didn't make a big deal, since he was a grown man, and likely didn't want to suffer the pink bellies and other indignities from the team that passed for birthday celebrations. But the Afghans said it was an insult in their culture not to throw a party for such an event. Colonel Agha said it was customary to have at least tea and cookies with your closest friends.

He practically ordered Tony to throw a party. The colonel said at first that he would withhold food from his men for three days, and when they asked why, he would tell them that when Tony threw a party, they could eat, and not before then.

But with Rza's help, Agha made a deal. If Tony didn't throw a party, the ANCOP could shave Rick's beard. Tony agreed, knowing full well that there would be no party, especially with missions on the horizon.

Meanwhile, nearby, Namatullah was scarfing down a peach, snatching leftover nuggets from the colonel's plate, and generally being a scavenger. Ever since we'd met and he'd tried to bribe the team into giving him more uniforms, I'd disliked the guy. There was something gutless about him. And he seemed more interested in himself than in his men. A cardinal sin for any officer. It was also disgusting to watch him eat. When someone would make a joke, he'd laugh, and food would roll out of his mouth.

With the Afghans finally running out of whiskey and the smoke cloud building in the trailer, the Russian made a last toast. With several drinks under his belt, he compared the ANCOP and Americans to bees.

"A single bee is not strong and can't make honey, but a hive is strong and makes honey," he said, Rza still translating. "The Americans and ANCOP are a hive with a common mission to rid Zhari of Taliban. All the world will taste our fucking honey."

CHAPTER 17

CHASING GHOSTS

Just before dawn, we headed out of the main gate of Camp Wilson and turned left onto Highway One.

The sun was just cresting the horizon and still hadn't burned off the haze covering the jagged mountains along the border of the Zhari and Panjwai districts. As I walked, I scanned the thick pomegranate groves and grape fields south of the highway. The landscape was picturesque, but I knew that inside the tangled vines and mud-packed mounds there were trip wires attached to IEDs. It was certain death if we stumbled upon any of them.

The day before, I'd traded in my cargo pants for an ANCOP uniform. With my helmet and pack, I looked like the rest of the tan walking along the road. When we'd reached Zhari, Gregg had pulled me aside and urged me to wear the uniform. Courtney had also backed the idea. Going out, as I'd been doing, dressed in a T-shirt and cargo pants made it harder for me to blend in with the team and the landscape.

"At least if they shoot at me first, I'm the least lethal person on the team," I said.

"Yeah, and then we can get their location from the direction of the shots," Gregg joked.

But the team's reasoning was simple and wise. If I looked different, I'd likely be a target. And my getting shot would put the team and mission in jeopardy. Gregg and the others would have to stop and treat me. And that violated my rule of being a seamless addition. I never wanted to dictate what and where the team went, because the minute I did anything like that, I was changing the narrative.

The night before, Matt told me a story he'd once read about a researcher who wore a gray wet suit and used to swim with seals off the coast of California.

"She was out in the water swimming with the seals when all of a sudden all of the seals disappeared," he said. "Then a great white shark, mistaking her for a seal, snapped her leg off. She bled out trying to swim back to shore."

So there was an inherent danger in both blending in and standing out.

After talking to a few reporter friends in Afghanistan, I decided to wear the uniform on the grounds that I'd be better protected. Plus, no one really thought the Taliban, if they started shooting at us, would skip over me because they could see I was a reporter. Not that it mattered, really, since my body armor was tan and I never wore the press patches you'd see dangling around journalists' necks. Even more, if we were captured, I didn't think the Taliban would honor my non-combatant status.

The night before, I tried on the uniform for the first time. No patches except for the ANCOP and Afghan flag. It felt strange to be in a uniform, but in some ways it was also transforming. I'd been slowly buying in and feeling more and more a part of the team. And now the uniform felt like it sealed the deal and changed my point of view. Forget about objectivity—at least as far as the Taliban was concerned. I was firmly on the American side. This, of course, was partly because it's hard to feel empathy for people who are trying to kill you, but it was also, simply, that I'd been with the team long enough now that it was hard for me not to see them as friends.

Marching down the highway, we were all weighed down with body armor, helmets, and packs filled with bottles of water and some snacks. Since my pack was much lighter than the others', the night before Matt had given me two fragmentation grenades, a smoke grenade to mark my position if we had to call in an air strike, and several M4 magazines. I'd asked for the additional gear figuring if we did run into a massive fight, I'd be around to at least make sure we didn't run out of ammo.

At this point, I'd also been given a pouch in which to carry Manny's unused radio. And I'd acquired another pouch to carry Gregg's small video camera, some pens and pads, and my earplugs. My body armor was slowly looking more and more functional.

As we walked down the highway, we were accompanied by two of the team's four armored trucks. I could see the remote-control guns scanning the tangled green of the fields and thickets to the south. The cameras mounted on both trucks' guns zoomed into the thick underbrush searching for fighters.

Courtney was helping to herd the ANCOP forward. Matt and Josh were at the front of the line. We were headed for a few compounds just south of the highway but well within sight of the base. Even though the 101st had been in country for more than five months, they'd never visited the compounds, and just days before the base had been attacked by a recoilless rifle near the cluster of compounds.

The patrol, the ANCOP's first in Zhari, was a practical way not only to help secure the base but also to give the police some on-the-job training. As we walked, Courtney told me about a late-night meeting he'd had with the 101st brigade commander. The latter, a colonel, had called Courtney up to his office around nine o'clock the night before the patrol because he wanted to hear how Courtney planned to use the ANCOP in the district.

"So he calls me into his office and says, 'So, tell me what you think I want to hear,'" Courtney began.

Courtney explained how the ANCOP cops would man the checkpoints along the highway and work out of the two bases they'd inherited from the brigade commander's men. The goal was to start building an accurate picture of the people in the district, identify power brokers, and begin "mapping" the population to win support. It was a classic Special Forces approach, one that focused on people first.

Courtney found out later that the colonel he'd just spoken with really didn't like Special Forces. He thought they were cowboys, and the meeting was really a dick-measuring contest to show the team that the colonel was still the commander around here, and it was he who was in charge of the battle space. The sad part was that the colonel wasn't proving much. He might own the battle space on a map, but the Taliban leaders were the true owners of the actual, physical land. They moved with some freedom in the villages south of the base and attacked with impunity. The only soldiers on the base who seemed to care, and who tried to fight back weren't even American. They were employees of Tundra, the Canadian security contractor, and their Afghan guards were the only ones who ever manned the walls.

So, while the day's patrol sounded like it was going to be boring and needless, it might also be one of the only times American soldiers and their Afghan counterparts ever set foot in the place. And it at least showed the Taliban fighters in the area that one unit was going to patrol.

Setting up the ANCOP in security positions around the compound, Josh, Tron, and Courtney led four ANCOP up to the door of the first compound. The door was a think piece of metal. The ANCOP soldier rapped on it a few times before a small, gray-bearded Afghan opened it. He saw the police and asked for a few minutes to get his women together.

I followed the clearing team into the compound a few minutes later and watched as Josh and Tron pushed the ANCOP soldiers in different directions. The compound was cramped with a massive tree growing near the side of the door. A cow was chewing some hay next to it, and several goats, with hay and twigs matted in their hair, were nibbling on some bark. Trash, yellow plastic jugs, and bits of crushed pomegranates littered the dusty ground. Every few feet, nuggets of goat shit covered the ground.

The farmer, whose name was Abul Hamid Khan, and his two sons sat on the edge of a well at the center of the compound.

ANCOP soldiers moved through the compound, searching. Josh stood nearby directing them as they passed from one room to another. The rooms were small and cut out of the mud walls. A dirty blanket covered the doorway, and several small children—both boys and girls—peeked out. When the ANCOP soldiers reached the final room, they stopped, because that was the room where the women were gathered.

"How many people live in the compound?" Tron asked.

"Three," Khan said through Rza. "Me and my two sons."

I noticed that he hadn't counted the women or children.

Tron pulled out a scanner to take the farmer's fingerprints and photo. This was an important part of building a picture of the human terrain. Using what was called the BATS system, Tron was able to take fingerprints and pictures as well as input data that would then be uploaded to a massive database. That way, if Khan should turn out to be an insurgent and was captured, the police would have his information. Mike the Cop liked to remind the team to get blood samples of any dead fighters so that their DNA could be checked against the database.

While Tron got the system ready, Courtney talked with the farmer, Khan.

"I have two small fields. One here by my house and other farther south," Khan said, gesturing with his hand toward his southern field.

"I don't work in the southern field anymore," he continued. "I don't feel safe. I am afraid of the guns."

He was referring to the artillery that rattled us out of bed.

With the BATS system up and running, Tron asked Khan his age. The farmer didn't know, but guessed that he was about fifty-five or sixty. He looked frail and crow's-feet creased his dark eyes. His skin was a tobacco brown, and wrinkled and leathery from spending hours in the sun. As he talked with Tron, his dirty, callused hands worked a string of worn brown worry beads.

Placing Khan's hand on the scanners, Tron tried to take his fingerprints, but the machine didn't work.

"Too many rough years and hard work," Courtney joked.

We all laughed, but Rza didn't translate the joke and Khan's face remained blank. The whole process was like voodoo to him. He had no idea what the machine did or why Tron—in armor and sunglasses—kept asking him questions. All he knew was that he couldn't work his fields because the base kept shooting shells into them.

Suddenly gunfire erupted east of the compound. It started and stopped at first like a sputtering engine, but for about thirty seconds there was sustained fire, including the pounding of a machine gun.

Courtney, his weapon ready in his hands, peeked out of the door of Khan's compound as he talked on the radio trying to see if anyone had seen who was firing. Rick, who had pushed his men up to a T-intersection farther down the road, said a kid came up and told him that the Taliban had instructed the residents of the village to stay out of the fields today.

"We're going to go down there and see if they want to play," Courtney said.

No people in the field usually meant an attack. With Tron now finished with the farmer, Courtney got the ANCOP in line and we hustled down to the intersection to link up with Rick and Mike the Cop near a canal.

"The kid said the men were in a field about three hundred meters south of here," Rick said, pointing to some fields that were separated by thick mud walls and irrigation ditches.

Rick's ANCOP soldiers were lined up on the canal aiming their rifles in the direction of the field. It was impossible to see anything. The underbrush was too dense and the fields were cut by dirt roads, deep canals with muddy bourbon-colored water, and massive grape huts that doubled as bunkers.

Before we pushed down into the field, Rick wanted to clear a compound nearby. Again with the ANCOP in the lead, we crept down the road. I found myself in the column on the right side of the road. As we got close, I squatted near the compound's well, near the canal, and watched as one of the ANCOP soldiers slowly walked up to the open door and knocked. Since the ANCOP soldiers don't need a warrant to search a compound, this soft-knock approach allowed the team to search any houses they wanted in order to root out the Taliban.

A well-groomed man came to the door. A small child, no more than three or four, was clinging to his long baggy light blue pants. Soon another, younger child with hair clipped short gripped his other leg.

He invited us into his compound and gave the ANCOP permission to look around. Unlike his older neighbor, Farmer Khan, Jamal Veddin, as this man was named, had a trimmed black beard and clean hands. His clothes looked new and he didn't have the same haggard and worn look as Khan had had.

While the ANCOP searched the compound, Veddin talked with Courtney and Rick while Rza translated.

"Does he have any farmland?" Courtney asked.

"Two orchards," Veddin replies. One was next to his house.

"Can you farm anytime you want?"

The Afghan shook his head. Pointing toward a police checkpoint, he told the captain that the Taliban often came to the village.

"They fire on the checkpoint while we're working on the farm," he said. "Then the police shoot back and hit my compound."

He told the captain that the Afghan National Police also shot at his compound for fun from time to time, damaging the wall. Veddin said when the ANP wasn't shooting, the American guns were. Veddin said that the Taliban laid their bombs in the road and in the fields, but right now the Americans were a greater danger. He was afraid to work in the fields because he had seen shells land nearby.

"They are going to kill everybody in the area," he said. "I don't want to be in the government, but I just want safety and to work my fields and stay with my family. We don't have a choice. This is the only house we have, with lots of women and children. We have nowhere else to go."

Courtney said he'd talk with artillery about the shooting, and assured the man that the ANCOP would be in the area.

"The best thing we can do is patrol this area," Courtney said. "Active patrols will keep the Taliban out and eliminate the need for the bombs and artillery."

Veddin told Courtney that he lived in this compound with his three brothers and their families. When Courtney asked how many women and children were living at the compound, he shrugged.

"A lot," he said.

In the short time we were there, I saw at least four children, including the two boys who clung on to Veddin's pants. The younger of the two kept a keen eye on me as I followed the conversation. Figuring I had a chance to lighten my load and do a good deed at the same time, I fished out two bottles of water and handed them to the boys. Only the younger one, the one watching me like a hawk, took the bottle. For the rest of the visit, he cradled it in both hands. He'd occasionally shake it, but never took a sip.

With the compound clear, we moved down the road and cut across the compound. Rick, and his ANCOP soldiers, were off to our left, moving through a field. Walking along the wall, I could see Matt and some ANCOP holding down the corner. We met up with him and he led us down to a second canal.

We slowly peeked out from the corner and scanned the field and a massive grape hut that overlooked the canal. A small footbridge crossed the first canal, and a second bridge, wide enough for a car, crossed the second, deeper canal. Matt immediately set two ANCOP soldiers up to watch the road. One was armed with a machine gun. They hunkered down and waited as Rick cleared the field to our left.

Moving back behind the corner, Matt and Courtney met up with each other.

"What a nut roll," Courtney said about the terrain.

"It would be great if we could get some high ground," Matt said, scanning the roofs of the surrounding compounds, hoping to spot a place to put a machine gun.

There was tension in the air. Everyone, including me, was waiting to get hit. And since it was impossible to see more than a few hundred meters, a group of Taliban fighters could've been lurking nearby. Squatting against the wall, I waited for the order to move across.

Rick and his ANCOP soldiers moved up first. We watched from the corner as they crossed the bridge and raced across to the other compound wall. After the last man in Rick's group passed, the captain and I followed. With us were Ben and John, the JTAC. If the fighting started, he'd be able to call in air support.

As we crossed the bridge, I got my first close look at the grape-drying hut. It was massive and stood more than three stories. Built with mud and rocks, it had slits cut into the walls to allow the hot dry air to pass through. Huts like this are perfect for snipers, who use them as fighting positions. A few years before, in the Panjwai district, the Taliban had used these huts as bunkers when Special Forces and Canadian soldiers were attacking the area. Unable to penetrate the walls with their guns, the soldiers had to use antitank weapons and a recoilless rifle to punch holes in them. The hut was a perfect fortification, and our patrol didn't have the kind of firepower needed to get through its walls.

Once they were across the canals, Rick and his ANCOP soldiers raced into the hut to clear it. With few soldiers across the canal, the captain, Ben, and John started pulling security. Two ANCOP soldiers set up, facing both ways down the road.

The field where the Taliban fighters told the boy to leave was just on the other side of the wall. It was large, with rows of grapevines growing on tan mounds of dirt. The grapes stretched out for about seven hundred meters to another cluster of compounds. There were no workers in the field and we sat looking over the wall and waiting.

While we waited for Rick to return, I heard the ANCOP soldier facing the west start yelling. There was a young man, of military age but probably no more than sixteen or seventeen, walking down the road. He was dressed in a brown *shalwar kameez* and had the traditional pillboxlike hat worn by the Pashtuns cocked to one side. He raised his arms as the ANCOP soldier pointed his rifle at him.

At this point, Courtney came over with Rza and started asking the boy questions. He was a farmworker, he told Courtney, and was headed home.

Courtney looked at his watch. It was still early morning. About nine o'clock.

"Why is he leaving so early?"

The kid told Courtney that he was done with work this morning.

"And he is going to come back to work later?"

The boy said yes.

But the story didn't add up. He might have buried his AK or put it back in the cache and was now content to just wait out the hostilities. Or maybe he'd been sent by his commander to see who was patrolling the area. Either way, his story of going home was likely bullshit and Courtney knew it.

Rick arrived moments later. He and his ANCOP cohort had cleared the grape hut.

They'd found nothing. It was empty.

Now everyone was looking over the wall where we were standing, searching for any sign of fighters. The boy was told to wait and stood with a blank look on his face as Courtney surveyed the field with the optic sight on his rifle. He didn't appear to be upset as he squatted near the wall under the watchful eye of an ANCOP with an AK-47.

We all wanted to find fighters there. We all wished they'd just pop up and try their luck. It was weird to hope that someone would just appear and start shooting at you. But it's what you want them to do at moments like that. By this point, we'd been walking for hours. The load of water and ammunition in our packs was digging into our shoulders. We were itching for a fight. Finding some insurgents would make the whole tiring patrol worthwhile. But in the back of your mind, you hope that if any of the enemy do happen to pop up, it will turn out to be a one-sided fight.

Matt suggested to the captain that we should shoot some smoke grenades into the field. If the fighters were hiding in it, maybe they'd start shooting, thinking that they had been attacked.

Both John, carrying an M203, which is an M4 rifle with a grenade launcher, and Rick, with a "bloop" gun, loaded a smoke grenade into the tube.

Bloop. Bloop.

Standing at the wall, we waited for the red smoke to appear. I saw a wisp of smoke from Rick's grenade first just off my right shoulder. It landed between some of the mounds, and immediately the smoke began to climb into the sky. John's grenade was a little harder to locate. Instead of hitting the field directly in front of him, it sailed and landed beyond the cluster of compounds.

"Hey John," Rick said. "You think maybe you can reengage and this time hit the field in front of you and not the mountaintop?"

John, with a sheepish green, loaded another grenade and fired it into the middle of the field. We waited for movement. Nothing. But as the red smoke dissipated, some plumes of gray and white smoke suddenly appeared. John had set the field on fire.

Courtney got on the radio.

"We're going to wait here for five minutes," he told the team.

Courtney didn't want to leave before he was sure that the fire wasn't going to spread and end up burning the whole field. In a war where winning over the populace was key, setting fire to their crops wasn't an especially strategic action.

"At least this time he hit the field," Rick said.

While we waited, some of the guys took pictures. It was obvious now that the Taliban fighters had decided to do something other than engage in an attack that morning. So while we waited for John's fire to go out, he took pictures of Jeremy, the team's junior medic, and Courtney. They joked that the pictures would soon find their way onto Facebook.

"My Facebook status should be 'currently out killing Taliban,'" Courtney joked.

Jeremy, after shooting a picture of John, said his status should be "Hi, I'm John. When I'm not out killing Taliban, I'm starting fires."

As the last wisps of smoke climbed into the sky, the captain ordered everybody to head back to camp. We slowly began marching, careful not to let our guards down. Matt again led the way. As we marched, we passed a massive marijuana field. The crop was dark green and more than head height. As we drew close, I could smell it. And truthfully, it smelled wonderful. Lush. Rich. Several of the guys stopped to pose for pictures. The field was a pothead's fantasy of heaven.

Back on Highway One, I saw Matt counting off the ANCOP soldiers.

"I thought we were going to see something today," Courtney said to Matt as we passed him.

"Yeah, me too," Matt answered, a look of resignation on his face. "But at the end of the day, a patrol is boots on the ground. And that is all that matters."

Turning back toward Wilson, I could finally feel the weight of my pack. My shoulder was sore and the pads in my helmet were soaked with sweat. But it felt good to be out, and for the first time in a long while, I felt like I'd found the war again. It would take more than one patrol to make a difference, but at least no attack had been launched on the base.

Back at Wilson, Courtney congratulated the ANCOP on a job well done. Gathering them around in front of their camp, he told them the patrol had been a big first step.

"Good job today. The Taliban was out there today, but they heard that the ANCOP were out there and got scared," Courtney told the soldiers as they huddled around him. "They got scared and that is the standard we need to set."

CHAPTER 18

TALIBAN BED-DOWN SITE

About a week after the recoilless-rifle attack, Fran was back.

He had information about a possible location from which the Taliban was launching attacks, and asked if the team and ANCOP wanted to check it out. Since his job was to protect the base, the mission fit into his duties. There was no way you could protect the inside of the base if you didn't get outside and see beyond its walls.

The night before the mission, Fran met with Courtney, Tron, Tony, and Rick in the operations center. As they huddled over a detailed map of the area, he told them that a captured Taliban fighter had pointed out two compounds in a village across the highway. Fran said that fighters were launching attacks from the nearest compounds and sleeping in the nearby village.

Standing in the back, I watched Fran set out the latest news and information on the Taliban in the area. He had better intelligence than anyone on the base and freely shared it with the team. He hoped that the Special Forces soldiers with their ANCOP would do a better job of building "white space"—military jargon for safe areas—around the base than the Regular Army was doing.

I marveled as Fran talked about what he'd done, and the risks he'd taken, in fulfilling the intelligence requirements of his contract. I could see how, with his thick black beard, he could pass as an Afghan in man-jams. Armed only with some grenades and a pistol, Fran had driven up and down Highway One on a motorcycle watching for Taliban. At least twice, he told the team, he had driven through a Taliban checkpoint. Both times, he ducked his head and mumbled as they waved him through, unaware that he was the enemy.

Courtney jumped at the chance to take the ANCOP on missions. The evening before the patrol, Fran drove out to the camp to talk with Courtney and Tron. Using a map projected on the plywood wall, Fran showed the Americans where he'd been before.

Fran had been down to where the Taliban was suspected of sleeping once with some of his Afghan guards. They had spotted fighters in the cluster of compounds during an attack. He said the Taliban put a spotter on top of one of the compounds who sent a runner to the shooter farther south. When he checked this information out a few days later, the locals told his guards to leave because there were fighters in the area. Fran's hope was that it would be possible to catch some fighters sleeping.

"It is going to be a busy year. They have nothing to do but fight," he said.

The patrol the team was about to undertake would be Courtney's first chance to think unconventionally. It was a daily wrestling match between him and the officers of the 101st over missions and over who had control over them. The 101st owned the area and they wanted to have control over the team. So, Courtney spent a lot of time at the headquarters making sure that the 101st understood the team's goals and that these goals matched those of the 101st.

Getting along with the 101st was the first Special Forces imperative: "Know your operational environment."

But it was a daily struggle since many conventional commanders thought the Special Forces teams were a bunch of cowboys who didn't follow the rules. That rift had been torn open in 2001 when the conventional side of the Army watched a few Special Forces teams and the CIA take down the Taliban. That's why Iraq was such a big invasion. The conventional Army wanted to remind policy makers in Washington that tanks and large groups of soldiers were valuable. It was the classic turf war to justify budgets.

But this mission was going to serve both the 101st and the captain. Courtney devised a plan to use the ANCOP's smaller Ford Ranger trucks to drive down to the village so that they could get to the compounds faster, and provide covering fire from the mounted machine guns.

We practiced loading and unloading the trucks the night before the patrol was scheduled since the plan was to leave Wilson at five-thirty in the morning, just as the sun rose, and surround the compounds. Afghans didn't move at night unless they had to because of the Americans' night-vision technology. The team also hoped to be in position before any civilians were awake because Fran told them that when the farmers who worked the fields saw the patrol, they'd alert the fighters so that the village wouldn't become a war zone.

As the engines of the trucks hummed, everyone looked toward the eastern mountains, waiting for the sun to rise. Since the rules of engagement made night missions almost impossible except for the highest-level targets, the team had to make sure they were operating at dawn, hence making the patrol a day mission.

With the sun's rays slashing across the valley, the trucks rolled out of the gate and turned west toward the compounds. The faint smell of pot hung in the air as we left, a smell everybody on my truck noticed right away. It wasn't clear who was doing the smoking, but it was a pleasant smell—a welcome break from the typical Afghan smells of sewage, animal waste, and burning garbage.

After a short ride down the highway, we reached the turnoff to the village. But what had looked like a road on the maps turned out to be a rutted goat track that John, the JTAC, could barely negotiate with the team's four-wheeler.

"It's all fun and games until someone loses a testicle," Mike observed as he hopped off the ANCOP Ranger truck. "I'd prefer to walk from here."

The trucks would never make it down the rutted path and Courtney didn't want to risk one getting stuck. Reluctantly, he sent the trucks back to camp and told the ANCOP soldiers to fan out and get ready to march.

Climbing out of the truck, I shifted my pack. My shoulders were already hurting. I'd changed my load since Matt decided to carry the Squad Automatic Weapon (SAW) instead of his M4. Matt had brought out the SAW in case we ran into the Taliban's tunnel system, which was rumored to be in the area.

To complement the machine gun, I was carrying hundreds of rounds plus extra grenades. Just as we were leaving camp, Tron had tossed me a tracking device that allowed friendly units to see us on the FBCB2, essentially a large Google map that showed the location of units on the battlefield.

It was never good when your shoulders hurt that early in a patrol. I knew that they'd go numb soon and then I'd be okay. But until then, they hurt as I shuffled my feet and waited. I resisted pulling on the straps or taking the pack off. I was relieved when Matt and Gregg finally pushed their group of ten ANCOP soldiers forward while Courtney, Rick, and Tony waited for the Afghans to take the machine guns off the truck. I was with the captain's group and waited.

As the ANCOP guys passed, Jeremy, the team's junior medic, helped one of the Afghans wrap a belt of bullets around his body.

"We need to get them bags or something," Rick said as we waited for the Afghans to finish. One of the drivers tried to give a machine gunner an MRE—Meal, Ready to Eat—but Courtney chased him off.

"Fuck no," he barked. "Let's go. We're taking too long."

We were losing time and needed to move. As the trucks drove back to Wilson, the Afghans and Americans disappeared into the tangled maze of compounds, wadis, and fields. The sun was quickly climbing into the sky and no one wanted to miss the Taliban, if they'd spent the night in the village.

Quickly crossing a dirt field, we took the goat paths through a few dry wadis that led to the edge of the village. Most of the fields were barren except for the marijuana plants. Unlike the head-high plants we'd encountered during the first patrol, this crop was smaller, but it was fragrant nonetheless. During one of the breaks, Rza asked Mike the Cop how much the plants were worth back in the United States.

"The government considers each plant to be worth two thousand dollars," Mike the Cop said. "They figure that's how much the plant will yield, when it matures."

When we got to the edge of the village, we met up with Matt. He was kneeling on the lip of a wadi looking into the village. Tron and Gregg had taken the ANCOP into a nearby compound, which they were searching.

"Are you tracking the guys on the wall?" Matt asked Courtney. "You go ahead and push your group straight up. There are fucking tons of dudes up there. There are four in the alley and then there are those guys up on the wall."

"All right," Courtney said, turning back to move the ANCOP forward.

Lined up and sitting along the wall of the village's mosque, there was a group of elders. Cloaked in long scarves against the early-morning chill, they watched the ANCOP climb out of the wadi and fan out. Right behind them, Courtney, Rza, and I marched up. Courtney stopped, pulled out his small notepad, and started talking to the elders.

"They are here to provide security," he said, gesturing to the ANCOP. "We are going to do a lot of local patrols to make this area safe."

The Afghans just nodded. They'd just finished their morning prayers when the team and ANCOP showed up.

"Who is the village elder here?"

A man dressed in sky blue baggy shirt and pants with a dark black beard spoke. He was acting as the group's spokesperson while the rest of the group seemed disinterested, staring off into the fields that surrounded the village or just looking through the ANCOP.

"The village elder passed away," the man said as Rza translated.

"How long ago?"

"More than two months," the man replied.

This was how it went on most patrols with the Afghans. After ten years of war, I am sure they'd all been asked the same questions over and over. And as each new unit arrived, I am sure that the new officer came and did the same thing as his predecessors. Staying on the fringe, I shot video of the men for a while and then watched the sun rise over the mountains. The fingers of light were filling the valleys of the taller mountains, spilling into the fields.

It really was a pretty morning. It was fall now and the oppressively hot weather was long gone, replaced by crisp mornings and nights. Afghanistan was really a beautiful place. I could see, standing outside the mosque, why the village men sat and watched the sunset here.

Nearby, Courtney was still talking. This was something that he had to do in order to better understand the area, but it was a painstaking task and required him to ask a question, wait for Rza to ask it in Pashto, and then wait for the answer to be translated back to him.

"Are they in the process of nominating someone to replace the elder?"

"They are not talking about that yet. They are going to sit and talk about it," Rza translated.

"How is the situation here as far as TB go?"

Watching Courtney talk, I noticed that one of the men in the group looked a lot like Karzai, the Afghan president. I wondered if his friends teased him, mock-blaming him for the corruption and ineptitude that plagued the government in Kabul. I could hear it now in Pashto: "Did you see your government's latest fuckup?"

"When was the last time they saw TB in this area?" Courtney asked.

"One month ago," Rza said. "They were using this road for traffic. They weren't harassing the people."

Before we left, the man who'd been talking asked Courtney why the Americans had bombed the village school. It was called the Yellow School, and they said the soldiers had destroyed it with their shells. More diplomacy delivered from the barrel of the howitzer. Courtney promised to ask about the school, thanked the Afghans for talking with him, and moved deeper into the village.

The village, if you could even call it that, was populated by a collection of farmers. The smell of animals hung in the air and goat shit was scattered on the trails and in the fields that we crossed. Most of the villagers were up and were heading to the market.

The ANCOP searched the compounds one by one. I stayed outside of most of them. Once you've seen one Afghan house, you've pretty much seen them all. Plus, I kept thinking that if it was my home that was being searched, the fewer guys walking around the better. So I stood and watched the Afghans get ready for the market.

While I waited for the team to finish searching a compound, I shot some more video of the village and of the Afghans sitting along the wall. Most of the Afghans just sat and stared at me. One kid, sitting away from everyone else, saw me shooting and covered up his face with his shirt. He had shaggy black hair and only wisps of hair for a beard. He looked like a young punk. The bravado and attitudes of the young are the same in Afghanistan as they are in the United States.

But there was something about the way this kid covered up. There was defiance, but there was something else as well. My mind immediately jumped to the conclusion that this kid was up to no good. Maybe he was a spotter for the Taliban, since this was one of the villages from which fighters fired at the base. I had no proof of what I was thinking, but for the first time in almost a dozen trips, I'd convinced myself that my intuition was right. But who was I? Just a civilian. This wasn't my war. In that moment, though, it was. Looking down at my uniform, I felt like I had chosen a side.

I kept shooting the kid even though he continued to cover his face. It was childish of me, but it was my way of fighting for my side. I didn't carry a weapon and had little to do but document the things around me. But in that moment I desperately wanted to *do* something, even if it meant making the young punk uncomfortable. Maybe when we left, he would tell his side about how the Americans had kept trying to shoot his picture and brag about how he'd kept his face hidden. In any case, as I slid my video camera into its pouch, I knew that my objectivity was gone. I was growing very comfortable with being a participant.

Nearby, Matt was talking to Gregg, who was searching a compound from which rockets had been shot weeks before. The compound was noticeably more affluent-looking than the others, with nice pillows and rugs, according to Gregg.

"On the compound you're in right now . . . on the rooftop, it is a confirmed spotting site for the rocket guys. If you can get up on that rooftop and look around to see if you can see anything . . ." Matt said.

Looking back toward Wilson, Fran was telling Courtney how the Taliban had shot rockets at the base from here.

"There were two spotters on the roof and a runner, and he was going back to the tall tree," Fran said to Courtney. "He'd beeline back and then he'd pop up back on the roof with the spotters, and they were probably just adjusting, but they were using a runner."

"Did they use a spotter here and the rockets were coming from farther south?" Courtney asked.

"Yeah. From further south. And there was a good three- or four-minute lag between the two. No sooner did he take off than woof, we'd get another round in," Fran said, using his finger to show the trajectory of the rocket.

From the village, you could see the corner tower, where Tundra contractors had seen the recoilless rifle days before. Fran said that since the 101st started their push south, they hadn't done anything in the village. The team and ANCOP were filling the void and cleaning up some bad PR—referring to the destruction of the school—to boot.

"The only thing they did was bomb the school," Courtney said.

It was half a joke, and it masked his disgust. The 101st was pushing deep into the district, but still had no idea what was going on in the villages closest to the highway and the base. It was like the ghosts of Vietnam all over again. Soldiers chasing phantom fighters through villages of farmers who cared little for the national security picture and only wanted to scratch a living out of the dusty fields.

"They bombed the shit out of it," Fran agreed.

"I'm going to talk with them to see if they did BDA," Courtney said.

BDA, or battle damage assessment, meant that you went back to look at what you'd just blown up.

"I guarantee they didn't," Fran said. "No one has gone down here."

Both men were sort of appalled by the bombing. It was unclear whether Taliban fighters had been hiding in the building, but whatever the case, destroying schools didn't lead to winning the populace. And if what I intuited about the young punk—who should have been in school—was right, that battle may already have been lost. Courtney was especially put out by the incident. This was the second time he'd had to apologize for the 101st. If they weren't shelling fields and scaring farmers, they were destroying schools.

"We are trying to at least bring something to this area. I'm going to put it in my sitrep and they're going to probably be a little bit hurt, but damn, they bombed a school," Courtney said. "The Taliban can use that as a huge IO campaign. A compound, that's one thing, but a damn school. Kids went to that school."

"And now there's nothing," Fran said. "You're not fighting the Germans or anything like that. They're not going to hole up in one position."

After the patrol, the team talked about the mission. A couple of lessons kept popping up. One, the constant shelling by the 101st wasn't stopping the Taliban; it was only making enemies out of the villagers because it made them afraid to leave their homes.

The second lesson was that few American or Coalition patrols were making it into the villages on a regular basis. The absence of Coalition patrols meant that Taliban fighters could set up spotters near the base and shoot rockets. The absence of white space made Camp Wilson an easy target.

But how do you win a "people-centric" war, a war that is fought among the people?

If Courtney had his way, he and the ANCOP would be out in the area every day talking and meeting the people. While the chitchat with the elders at the start of the patrol we'd just finished seemed like the same song and dance that other patrols sang and danced, it was a first step toward forging the kind of relationships that would be needed in order to eventually build a new school and hopefully acquire some information that would lead the team to the Taliban.

CHAPTER 19

STANDOFF

Since the construction of the checkpoints was behind schedule and the 101st needed troops in order to push south, it was decided to give the ANCOP an outpost near the highway.

The outpost—called Pulchakhan—was located just south of Highway One. The walls were made of Hesco barriers. The outpost was built around some existing white buildings, with its towers made of plywood and sandbags.

The outpost sat on a dirt road that bisected two graveyards. The road, which was highly traveled by locals, was one of the main routes used by trucks and motorcycles moving from the villages. The idea was to put the ANCOP there so that they could set up a checkpoint and the team could launch patrols into the nearby villages.

A few days earlier, the team had visited the outpost with Colonel Agha. They'd toured the barracks rooms, the makeshift command post, and the towers that overlooked the road on one side and a small village on the other. A young platoon leader showed Courtney, Rick, and Tony around. At the time, soldiers from the 101st and Afghan soldiers were living together. They didn't patrol because of a lack of men, and were essentially just holding ground.

The camp was in decent shape, except for an older compound that was in the process of being torn down. Its mud-walled rooms and courtyard were covered in trash. And a burn barrel that was belching thick, nasty smoke made the place unbearable.

But overall, everyone was excited to be there. There was a village nearby and Courtney liked being far from Wilson and deeper into the district, where he knew he could make a difference. After this first visit, Agha had agreed to base some of his ANCOP soldiers in the outpost while the 101st and their ANA partners packed up to leave.

Finally, moving day arrived and the team planned to spend the night at the outpost and then patrol the village early the next morning. When we arrived late that afternoon, Courtney wasn't pleased with what he saw.

First, he noticed several ANCOP out of uniform or standing on top of the towers at the checkpoints. Grabbing Namatullah, he pointed out the problems to him. It was one of the few times that the ANCOP executive officer had left Wilson. Certainly it was the first time I'd seen him since the dinner hosted by Colonel Agha. He mostly stayed in the ANCOP camp.

"The guy in the tower didn't even have a weapon. I can't trust guys like that to walk with me on patrol," Courtney said. "I'm just trying to keep your guys alive and bring all my guys home."

Namatullah seemed annoyed that he'd had to leave Wilson at all and didn't at first respond to the reproof.

"When they find out someone is coming over, they will put their uniforms on," he finally said.

Wrong answer, as was evident by the stern look on Courtney's face. This was a matter of discipline. Discipline and an aggressive security posture in a war were what saved lives, and Courtney wanted the ANCOP to be doing the right thing even when no one was watching.

"If I was an insurgent, I would hit them," Courtney said. "It doesn't take but a few guys to roll up in a Jingle truck."

Namatullah shrugged and sulked over to his men, yelling at them to get their uniforms on and to grab their weapons.

Courtney turned his attention to the outpost, which did nothing to improve his mood. The place was a mess. Garbage was piled up next to barrels, the strips of flypaper hanging in the headquarters room were covered with bugs, and there was a pile of rotten potatoes in a corner of the storeroom where the ANA kept its food.

The outpost was built around a large building that contained several rooms. On one side of the building, there was a small operations center and an area where the team set up some cots. On the other was a large bay with bunk beds and cots used by the ANA.

The Afghan side of the building was covered in the ANA soldiers' detritus. Scattered around the room were boots and trash and I noticed a stink that seemed to seep out of the room. Next to the sleeping area was a small room with two refrigerators and a freezer. Three storerooms made up the perimeter. One stored MREs. The other two, used by the ANA for supplies, were empty except for the potatoes.

Outside, there was an air-conditioned tent with cots and two small buildings. One was used as a med station and the other was a kitchen. The med station was rudimentary at best, and dirty. Gregg was upset when he saw it and spent time looking for the medics so that he could impart some wisdom.

Besides the trash in the barracks and storerooms, there were large piles of trash outside the buildings, and the Porta-Potties were full. The smell hung in the air like a storm cloud, and even at ten feet away, the stench burned your nostrils. Everyone kept their distance as they walked around the camp. Word came out later that the Afghan who drove the shit-sucking truck had been killed a few days before and a replacement hadn't been found yet.

In the meantime, though, nothing was being done to fix the problem.

On paper, the camp was perfect and located far enough south to allow the team to start mapping the human terrain in the village. All morning I'd talked to Courtney, Matt, and Gregg about the opportunities the camp presented. It offered a perfect way to expand patrols in the area, and the captain, who was always on the lookout for a location for a Village Stability Operations site, loved it. It would have been even better if had only been located farther south. All the same, it gave the team its own camp away from Wilson and closer to the people. Plus, the village nearby was a perfect site to start reconstruction projects.

But the way the 101st and their ANA allies left the camp was embarrassing. The defense had always been that an Afghan solution was better than an American one. A rule stolen from T. E. Lawrence— better known as Lawrence of Arabia—and one of the best at building rapport and leading an insurgency. He was really a Green Beret before they even existed.

While the rule holds true for some things, it didn't apply here. A dirty camp was a dirty camp. It was the same in Pashto as it was in English. And the state of the camp wasn't really an Afghan solution. To Courtney, the issue was discipline and proper soldiering. And undisciplined soldiers are usually dead soldiers.

Everybody knew that the only way for the United States to get out of Afghanistan was by creating a strong Afghan Army. The 101st called their effort to achieve this *shonna ba shonna*, translated as "shoulder to shoulder." Their plan was to pair every Afghan soldier with a U.S. counterpart in order to enhance the locals' training.

On a dry-erase board in the outpost someone had written several Pashto words. The 101st loved to talk about how they worked shoulder to shoulder with their Afghan allies. But Rick said all of that was more show than substance. He called it a false bond that wouldn't survive the current deployment. The 101st's failure to enforce basic standards at the outpost showed that they didn't really care about their Afghan partners.

"Just look at the little things. If they truly cared about them, they would have stopped this right off the bat," Rick said to me as we walked around the dirty camp. "We try and nip it in the bud right away."

What the 101st had done was essentially an example of the conventional military borrowing a move from the unconventional side, but doing so with little understanding and even less success. Just partnering and talking about being "shoulder to shoulder" wasn't sufficient. What made the Green Berets special was their ability to build rapport. As Rick and I looked around the camp, it was clear to us that *shonna ba shonna* was just words. Just like the handful of Pashto ones written on the whiteboard. They were words to be learned and parroted back to officers and reporters when needed. But no one in the 101st seemed to believe them. And even if they did, the fact was, they weren't instilling any of the skills the Afghans needed to make them a good fighting force. That much was evident from the shameful condition of this camp.

"We understand what it means to be partnered, and letting the ANA do whatever they want and trash a base is not being a partner. The Regular Army doesn't care about their indig," Courtney said.

Outside, both the Afghans and the American soldiers in the 101st were eager to leave. Their trucks were lined up and ready to drive back to Howz-e-Madad. I heard several talk about getting back to the base in time to take a shower and grab a hot meal.

Standing nearby was the team. The grumbling was quickly turning into anger. After asking both the 101st and the resident Afghans to clean up to no avail, Courtney had had enough of the excuses and the lack of discipline and accountability.

Spotting the Afghan Army unit's first sergeant, he marched over to him.

"Hey, before you leave, pick up that trash and take it out," Courtney said to the soldier, a lean man with dark skin and a neatly trimmed beard.

The first sergeant was wearing sunglasses and the ANA's green beret, a tribute to their first trainers, some Fort Bragg–based Green Berets. He walked with a swagger and barely looked at the captain as he answered.

"We don't have any trash bags," was all he said.

"Then get some," Courtney told him. "If we were ripping out, we would not leave this place like you're leaving it. You will not leave it like this."

The Afghan tried to ignore Courtney, waving him off with his hands. This dismissal pushed Courtney over the edge. He snatched the Afghan's beret and threw it in the dirt. Then he grabbed the Afghan's fake Oakley sunglasses and threw them onto the ground.

The Afghan froze.

His eyes were huge. Stunned by Courtney's reaction, and by the way he was yelling at him, he just stood there. Behind him, a few of the Afghan soldiers slid magazines into their M16s.

Tony, who'd been watching the whole exchange, pushed Courtney away before he threw a punch. Courtney was shaking he was so angry. It wasn't just the garbage that had set him off. It was the disrespect. The fact that the Afghan thought it was okay to blow off an officer and not even show him the courtesy of looking him in the eye.

"I am frustrated by these fuckers," Courtney said as he walked away.

Rick, who was standing with me in a crowd of ANCOP, watched as more Afghan Army soldiers loaded their weapons. He caught Matt's eye and signaled for him to watch out. Soon word was passed among the team and everybody had their weapons slung across their chests. The team hung close to their trucks while the Afghan Army soldiers loaded up their Humvees and trucks in preparation for leaving.

It was a standoff.

Both sides were mean-mugging each other. I was standing between Gregg and Matt in front of the first Afghan Humvee. As the Afghans loaded, I could tell that Gregg and Matt were coming up with a plan of action just in case all hell broke loose. Day, one of the other team members, was hanging on to the other side of the team's truck out of sight of the Afghans. He was planning to flank the Humvee with other members of the team.

"I'm going for the SAW gunner in the turret," Matt said, keeping an eye on the Afghan soldiers as they loaded up.

"I'll go to the left," Gregg said.

Seeing that I was in the line of fire, I told Matt that I was going to move out of the way.

"You're probably safer here," Matt said. "I'm sure these guys can't shoot."

While the Americans continued planning for the worst case, the Afghans stared at them with hateful looks. One sergeant, who was the first to slide a magazine into his rifle, kept glaring in the direction of Matt and Gregg. I spotted a few Afghans reenacting the confrontation between the captain and the sergeant for those who hadn't seen it.

Everybody kept a keen eye on the first sergeant who'd been dressed down. He mostly kept out of sight, sitting in the lead Humvee's passenger seat, pouting. Finally, the last of the Afghan soldiers got to the convoy and the trucks slowly rolled out of the gate, leaving most of the trash at the camp. A few 101st soldiers had gone around and picked up some of it, but none of the Afghan Army soldiers offered to help.

As the Afghans cleared the main gate, Gregg and Matt stood in the open and watched each truck go by.

"My shit was on fire," Matt said as the last truck went by.

He'd been sure that the gunfight he'd been waiting for was going to happen, a fight between two "friendly" forces. The irony of the situation was not lost on Courtney, who, at the evening meeting, apologized for the incident.

"I was concerned about your safety, but I don't take 'go fuck yourself' lightly," he said. "From the way he spoke to me, he thought I was like the Regular Army. It was straight 'Fuck you. We're not cleaning up.'"

But there was no need for apologies. Courtney's actions were looked on favorably by the team, who saw it as an example of their leader standing up for them. They instantly had his back and had been ready to mix it up with their so-called allies without hesitation.

CHAPTER 20

PX RUN

After an uneventful patrol, the team returned to Camp Bohle.

A few days later, they had to go back to Kandahar Airfield to pick up some supplies. I decided to tag along and took a spot next to Gregg in the rear hatch of a truck. I had also promised Ben that I'd get him some dryer sheets from the PX.

The drive from Wilson to KAF only takes about an hour, but it offered a great opportunity to see the beauty of Afghanistan. From the gate of Wilson to the Arghandab River crossing, all you could see from the back of the RG were fields and open desert.

Settling into the seat, I scanned the farms and orchards. In the distance, I could see the two mountains that formed the natural boundary of the district. In the morning light, they looked majestic and the green of the grape fields was vibrant with life. Afghanistan was stunning.

On the trip, I realized that even on small Special Forces teams, groups within the group had a way of forming. I'd fallen in with Gregg and Matt almost from the start. I'd eat dinner with them, poke around the shops near the Bohle gate with them, and borrow movies from Gregg's collection downloaded on a portable hard drive.

It was funny how Gregg's taste meshed with mine. We shared a love of all things Indiana Jones. Many of his favorite books were also favorites of mine. I borrowed and read two of his books during the trip. Both had been on my reading list at home.

As for Matt, we were both fans of the Boston Red Sox and had suffered through a tough season together. Matt, a catcher in high school, had even brought a pair of gloves and some baseballs to Afghanistan. A couple of times we threw in the motor pool. With Afghan countryside as our backdrop, he grooved throw after throw into the glove, snapping the leather.

One evening, we got the metal softball bats out and collected up some pomegranates from an orchard near the camp. Standing only a few feet away, Matt lobbed a fruit underhand to Josh, who, with a long left-handed swing, crushed it.

Matt dug in next. Josh tossed a second fruit high. Matt waited and was able to get the barrel of the bat on the pomegranate, sending pieces of it in all directions and splattering his face with bits of pulp and juice. Josh's next pitch was lower and the impact covered Matt's shoes with pomegranate.

I hit third. Josh's pitch was straight down the middle and I hit it square, spraying the now-gathering crowd with juice.

"This is like the shit in *Good Morning, Vietnam*," Josh joked.

The last batter was Ray, a new interpreter. He was born in Afghanistan but lived in New York and had come back to make some money. Josh's pitch was high, and Ray whiffed. A loud roar went up from the crowd.

Josh pitched again and Ray hit the pomegranate on his second try, but no one remembered that. For the rest of the night, they only remembered the swinging strike.

So, as I climbed into the truck with Gregg it was just an extension of the conversation about the war and the future that we'd been having for weeks. Since I often rode in Matt's truck, I hadn't spent a lot of time on missions with Gregg.

As we motored down the highway, I noticed that Gregg made it a point to wave to all the kids, especially the girls in their vibrantly colored dresses.

"You know I've never seen a girl beg us for stuff," he said as he waved to a small girl in a green dress. The neckline was decorated with an intricate pattern of yellows and reds.

The boys were another story. If they waved, Gregg said, it was usually followed by a request for a pen, water, or food.

Under the Taliban, life was hard for women. We often saw them walking under their burkas, looking like ghosts. If they were alone, the men and boys barely seemed to notice them. The girls who were brave enough to go to school sometimes got acid thrown in their faces.

For Gregg, the war was pretty simple.

"If we were only here so that little girls could go to school, sign me up," he said.

As we got closer to the city, the chatter stopped and Gregg started to focus on the now-crowded streets.

The real danger on the convoy to KAF was the leg between Wilson and the outskirts of Kandahar. The team had made contact once on the way to Wilson, but this had happened only that once. Still, the drive was dangerous, despite the 101st's best efforts to push the enemy south. The interlocking compounds that were a feature of the area offered great hiding spots.

All of the drainage pipes were covered by concertina wire and the bridges had checkpoints to protect against the bombs, but going over both was still a tense moment. As the truck's tires hit the bridge, I held my breath. Every time we crossed, I held my breath. It wasn't something I thought about it. I just did it.

Luckily, we crossed the bridge into Kandahar without incident. Once across, we moved through the Afghan version of a "Flying J Travel Plaza." Trucks lined the road. Drivers slept underneath their vehicles or gathered near their hoods to have tea and talk.

The traffic behind us (we were the last truck) suddenly picked up as we headed toward the center of Kandahar City. Motorcycles and cars tried to get past us, but Gregg quickly waved them off.

"Hey," he barked, holding his hand up to halt the driver. "Stay back."

One Afghan on a motorcycle kept pressing his luck. After every speed bump, he crept closer. Each time Gregg waved him off, the motorcycle driver shot us the peace sign.

"Don't give that peace sign. Stay back!" Gregg said, using his best cop voice from his days on the Madison, Wisconsin, force. "That motherfucker wants to get shot."

Once, a black sedan didn't stop, prompting Gregg to grab his M240 machine gun. The driver saw this and skidded to a stop.

"He is cleaning his man-jams right now," I said as we both laughed.

At the major intersections of the city, Afghan traffic cops in green uniforms and white hats did their best to manage the chaos, but while watching one work, Gregg and I couldn't for the life of us figure out what practical effect he was having on the melee of cars, motor bikes, donkey carts, tractors, and motorized rickshaws.

One busy motorist in a white Corolla found his way behind two green ANP Rangers. Gregg waved the Afghan cops by, but told the driver of the Toyota to stop. The man, whose face was covered by the windshield, threw his hands up and pointed at the ANP trucks and then back at him like he was a cop.

"Hey bro, I don't know you," Gregg yelled back. "You should have put on your uniform and gone to work today."

The gate leading into Kandahar Airfield was crowded with trucks hauling supplies. I noticed an old Afghan MiG sitting in the median. Nearby, an Afghan guard stood under the shadow of the wing reading a newspaper. We made the turn and slowly followed the mix of military trucks and Jingle trucks into the base. It had been a dusty ride, and Gregg and I hurriedly ducked inside the truck to avoid the dust cloud kicked up by the tires and enjoy some shade. Overhead, the afternoon sun was heating up.

After spending time at Wilson, which felt like we were at war, Kandahar Airfield looked like an ugly American city filled with lots of European tourists. Soldiers from a handful of nations, thanks to NATO—the Netherlands, the UK, Canada—walked around unarmed and apparently unfazed by the war that was being waged around them. Overhearing their conversations, I got the feeling that their most serious concern was a shortage of coffee at the French PX.

But for the guys who were having to do without, like the soldiers at Camp Wilson, a PX run was a treat. Parking the trucks, the team peeled off their gear and bounded across the street into what can only be compared to a Walmart at home. The warehouselike building was filled with junk food, sodas, magazines, and even obnoxious T-shirts advertising Operation Enduring Freedom.

Only Americans would make T-shirts for a war.

Gregg and the others had shopping lists and soon spread out to search for what they needed. Others, like Rick and Jeremy, just wandered around the aisles. I did the same, enjoying the air-conditioning and the chance to kill some time in a familiar American retail setting. I only spent a few minutes before I picked up the dryer sheets and left. When I got back outside, the team was done shopping and voted against staying for lunch. It was better to just get back to the camp. A short trip to the PX and a glimpse of the state of Kandahar were enough.

Suiting up again, we headed across the base to Camp Simmons, located next to Kandahar. Just outside, Dave had the trucks piled high with supplies. He, Josh, and some of the other team members were waiting for us outside the gate. Josh took a moment to greet the team. He was shocked when Gregg told him that Wisconsin, Gregg's alma mater, had beaten Ohio State.

"You're joking," Josh said.

Gregg wasn't, and soon Josh started to focus on what Wisconsin's victory meant for Alabama.

"That means Boise State is probably number one. That means my beloved Alabama has a chance with one loss," Josh said, looking up into the crystal-blue sky and scratching his chest.

He was, of course, wearing a crimson Alabama T-shirt.

While we were waiting to go, the B-team returned from their mission. They'd been out in Panjwai, a nearby district for the last several days. It was a Taliban stronghold and there'd been a big push by the commandos to clear the area of fighters.

But the success of the mission came with a price.

At Simmons, the team learned that a medic on a 20th Special Forces team had been wounded by an IED. He was alive, but had lost both legs and one of his arms.

Everybody got quiet.

"He was a good dude," Gregg said.

For the next several minutes, no one said anything. They seemed to be grappling with what this news meant. Gregg was the one who was hit the hardest. The wounded medic was an instructor and had helped train Gregg. He was from Chicago, and between training sessions they bonded over the Cubs.

For the rest of the day, Gregg was in a funk. His constant sarcastic commentary, for once, came to a halt. He was too upset to be thinking about anything else but his buddy and about how nonchalant the team seemed to be taking the IED threat.

"To me, it bears testament to what I've been saying about IEDs. If they're going to get us, this is how they are going to do it," he said. "I don't want to see my friends with their legs blown off. I don't want to get my legs blown off."

The hour-long ride seemed longer on the way back. Even my thoughts drifted to the randomness of war, where even good dudes got a raw deal. Afghanistan no longer looked beautiful to me. It was just a hot and dangerous place where good dudes could be maimed for life.

And for once I didn't feel silly holding my breath on the bridge. It had kept me safe so far.

CHAPTER 21

RUINS

Before we left the dusty base just south of Pulchakhan, Courtney gathered the team together.

As the guys huddled around him, he took out his map and, using a knife as a pointer, showed the team the route to a particular village. The mission was simple. We were headed to a village not far from the 101st base in Lako Khel.

The 101st soldiers were well into their offensive to push from Highway One to the Arghandab River. While they cleared the villages, engineers paved a new road from the highway. They were based at Lako Khel, where the engineers spent the day moving up and down the new, dusty road while the infantry patrolled. In the distance, I heard the rumble of explosions as the engineers blew their way through the walls that lined the Afghan fields.

But with all the troops pushing south, the 101st's flanks were exposed. And so Courtney proposed taking the ANCOP out to the villages to check for fighters and to make contact with the locals. The goal was to make sure that insurgents weren't just moving away from the patrols and hiding in places the 101st had already cleared. And Courtney also wanted to continue to build an accurate picture of who lived in the district.

Before we left the base, Courtney gave us an update on the latest intelligence. A few hours before, an IED blast had showered some 101st soldiers with shrapnel, but didn't wound any of them severely.

"They took some potshots from the cluster of these compounds," Courtney said, tapping his knife on the map as he talked. "Some harassment fire. That's it."

"Did they say what compound they took fire from?" Rick asked.

The captain pointed to a cluster of buildings on the map where the 101st suspected the Taliban fighters were.

"They've been here about two weeks and no one has been over there," Courtney said.

The team still didn't have a bomb-sniffing dog. One was on the way, Tony said during one of the nightly meetings. But this news didn't make anyone feel better.

"Remember to keep the Afghans out in front and check for signs of IEDs," Courtney said.

"Yeah, watch for those blown-up ANCOP," Matt said. "That is a good sign of IEDs."

The joke got a little laugh.

The patrol's planned path took us through a cluster of ruins. Changing the plan on the fly, the team picked out a new route that bypassed the ruins and showed it to Matt.

"We don't need to fuck around with the ruins because they are fucking ruins," Courtney said.

Gathering up the ANCOP soldiers, Matt, Gregg, and Tron led the way out of the camp.

"Just beat feet up the road and take a right," Matt said. "Just take it slow."

Soon we were all on the road. Massive trucks hauling supplies caked us in dust as they passed. Just before we turned off the main road, an Afghan boy, no more than fifteen years old, slowly weaved through the line of ANCOP soldiers on his bike. Nearby, an American truck drove by. All the while the kid seemed oblivious to the war around him.

The patrol stopped just on the outskirts of the village, where Matt and Courtney met up. The ruins formed a maze of mud-packed walls that made for perfect ambush sites. Even though the place was deserted, according to the 101st, Matt wanted to be cautious.

"We'll push up and fucking rally in the middle, right there," Matt said, pointing to a break in the compound walls, "and continue to push."

When we got to the village, it was empty, which often meant trouble. Moving through a break in the wall, we crossed a field that hadn't been tended in a while and over a small thigh-high mud wall. Up ahead sat a massive grape hut. All I could think about was where I would be able, if necessary, to find cover in the open field. Crossing at a half trot, I kept my distance from the others and hoped that a Taliban gunner wasn't training his weapon on us.

Safely on the other side of the field, we cut down a narrow alley between two compounds. The walls were tall and smooth, creating a shaded area that offered a short reprieve from the sun. It was hot, but not as hot as the summer heat that often topped out at a hundred degrees. Even after I'd walked only a short distance, my shirt was wet and I needed to take a few sips of water.

Off in the distance, we could hear gunfire. At first, it was just a few pops. But soon it built into a steady roll of rifle fire punctuated by the rattle of machine guns. Hoping to catch the fighters in the open, we hustled toward the sound of the guns.

On the way, I noticed Rza shaking his head. He seemed weary of the fight. His body language seemed to say that he was resigned to the fact that there could be fight, and he seemed tired of the violence. This was the guy who had killed more people than an epidemic of smallpox, according to the team. The man who told me, without emotion, that he'd cut down a half-dozen Taliban fighters in a market with one long burst from his SAW.

"They can make this life easier without fighting by being friends with each other. Be nice with each other. It would be better," Rza stated.

Picking our way along a wall, we hustled to keep up the pace. The gunfire was getting closer and it sounded like more fighters or soldiers had joined the fight.

"You've been fighting a lot of years, haven't you?" I said to Rza as we trotted behind the ANCOP.

"I kill more people than all my family members," Rza said. "Seriously, I am tired of killing people."

On the other side of the ruins, we perched on a wall overlooking some fields and listened. Courtney didn't want to rush into a fight. While he worked the radio to see where other friendly forces were located, we waited.

"Hang tight right here," Courtney said. "If they break contact, maybe they'll push our way."

Meanwhile, back in the village, Matt and Tron noticed that some of the compounds were locked. Using Matt as a human ladder, Tron and Habib climbed onto the roof with some ANCOP. The Afghans saw tail fins of a rocket and jugs that could be used to hold explosives. Climbing down into the structure, they found a block of TNT, an antipersonnel mine, which Dave said was big enough to blow off someone's leg, and several sleeping mats.

While Tron searched the compound, Courtney and Mike decided to go back into the ruins and search the other compounds whose doors were locked. Rick, Josh, and Tony's team of ANCOP waited at the wall. By now, the fire had become more sporadic and seemed to be quickly fading away. But the team wasn't sure if the fighters were headed toward us, so they stayed in place to protect us while the other groups searched the compounds.

Gathering up their ANCOP, Courtney and Mike weaved back over the ditch and field. The first compound had a green metal door. While Mike looked on, Rza gave it a few short, swift kicks. In a few seconds, the rusty hinges broke.

With the door hanging by a single broken hinge, the ANCOP went in and started searching. The main door opened into a courtyard. Inside, there were five smaller rooms. A storage area was directly in front of the door. All of the doors to the rooms were open, except the last one on the right. Mike shattered the wooden door with one kick.

"Door's open," he said, peeking inside, and then sending in an ANCOP to search the room.

The compound was littered with trash. It was hard to see the dirt floors in the rooms because they were covered in junk. Old parts of bikes, cooking bowls, and paper. Jeremy found a pile of prescriptions, some in English, which he folded into his pocket to show to Tron. The prescriptions had names written on them. The ANCOP found an old Koran, which they picked up and held on to, telling Courtney they wanted to take it to a safe place.

The first compound was a dry hole, but something about the place didn't sit right with Mike.

"There is something else here," he told the captain.

"I know. Just look at what Tron found," Courtney said.

"Yeah. And I'm not going to be trumped by a Mexican," Mike said, joking about Tron's nationality as he led the ANCOP to the next locked compound. Rza again shattered the door and Mike and the Afghans, with Jeremy, began the search.

Courtney went back to the wall on the eastern side of the village to call in the find. Meanwhile John and Josh had set up a satellite antenna. Courtney radioed back to the headquarters at Wilson he was going to blow the cache in place. It was too dangerous to carry it out, and he didn't want to leave it for the Taliban.

With permission to blow it, Dave set charges on the TNT and the mine. Moving to the outskirts of the village, he set them off, sending a cloud of smoke into the air. The smoke billowed out of the compound and floated up into the sky. When Rick saw Dave, he asked if this was his first time using explosives.

"Yeah, on the team," Dave said.

"Case of beer," Rick said.

Afterward, Courtney went back to do a battle-damage assessment. The room where the explosives had been found was now a pile of rubble. Unusable. Tron threw a grenade on a suspected spotter's site at a nearby compound, collapsing the roof.

Instead of pushing into the nearby village, Courtney and Rick decided to wait a few days and see what effect the blowing of the cache had on the area. Back at Camp Bohle, Courtney got an e-mail from the 101st brigade's military intelligence shop. They had known that the ruins were a possible staging area for Taliban fighters, but hadn't planned any kind of operation to check them out.

"Not sure what they are waiting for since you can see the ruins from their base," Matt joked that night at dinner.

A few days later, Courtney got another e-mail from 101st battalion, which was in charge of the area. The message blasted him and the ANCOP soldiers for running "unauthorized patrols." There had been an ongoing struggle between the team and the 101st battalion almost from day one. Among other things, the officers of the 101st had complained that they didn't have the team's radio frequencies.

The latest e-mail struck a nerve both because it was off base, and because it seemed to have more to do with some rift between the American units and the ANCOP and ANA than with the SF team. The day that Tron and the ANCOP found the weapons cache near the base, the ANA commander had been upset that the ANCOP soldiers were going out on patrol.

A few days later, the team drove out to the 101st battalion's base at Howz-e-Madad. After we arrived, Josh worked on the radios at the unit's operations center. He found and filled an unused radio with the team's frequencies, despite the battalion's claims that they didn't have any more radios.

While Josh worked, Courtney and Tony went over to meet Major White, the unit's operations officer, to iron out their differences.

Courtney was upset with White because of the nasty e-mail he had sent about the patrol without trying to work things out with him first. Plus, all of the information White had complained about not having had been submitted in the operations brief.

"My concern is that we don't complement each other," White said. "We don't know if you're there and we're there at the same time."

This, of course, was absurd since White had received the operations brief well in advance and knew the team was going to do the patrol near Pulchakhan.

White went on to complain that they didn't know the team's radio frequency and couldn't raise them on the radio. This, again, was absurd since the frequencies were included in the operations plan.

But Courtney played it cool.

"We have our own frequency, team internal. When you need us, you can bump up to our frequency," he said.

But White wasn't playing along.

"We took your con-op up to the TOC. The bottom line is that we're not tracking like we should," he said. "You are limited to the number of radios you can carry and I am limited on the number of radios we can monitor. Right now we have seven."

"We don't want to point fingers," Courtney said. "We'll work through this, sir."

Courtney made it clear that the team would continue to push into the villages trying to find a suitable place to set up a VSO site.

"That is why we need to get out to the villages—to see where they can support the site instead of just throwing a dart at the map," Courtney said. "As you guys patrol down south, I want the ANCOP down there to patrol. We are essentially watching your six."

CHAPTER 22

A MAGIC PILL

Medical care was one way of reaching the people.

Gregg, Jeremy, and Josh tried to organize a medical clinic in District 9, but it never happened because of the changing mission. So, the village near Pulchakhan was selected as the perfect site to try to set one up in Zhari.

Courtney had already talked to the village elder during a previous patrol and had to go back and meet with him again about starting the project. Assuming that Courtney would be tied up for a while talking, Gregg and Jeremy packed extra medical supplies and figured they'd treat some of the villagers while Courtney worked.

Arriving at the village, the team set up the trucks on the outskirts. A cluster of compounds near a wadi overlooked some fields; the village had a main drag that ran from the wadi past two large compounds and into more fields on its opposite side.

Courtney, along with Rick and Tony, met the elder under a tree near the wadi and started to talk. Grabbing my video camera, I tagged along with Gregg and Jeremy, who set up about halfway down the main drag. After laying a blanket near the mud wall on one side of the compound, they set down their packs and started to take out supplies.

Sitting on a portable camp chair, Gregg unzipped his med kit. Heavy even by the toughest standards, the bag was packed with over-the-counter painkillers, vitamins, and other simple remedies. In Afghanistan, Gregg said, people wanted presents. Like a goody bag at a kid's birthday, he had something for every patient even if it was just a vitamin-B capsule.

It didn't take long for the Afghans to crowd around. The first patient was a young boy whom I recognized as someone Jeremy had tried to treat during an earlier patrol. He had a serious spinal deformation that made his back bow backward like a letter C and pushed his chest out in an almost grotesque way. Despite the deformation, the boy seemed in good spirits, and when I saw him on the patrol he'd given me a huge smile.

This same smile he now shot Gregg. Pulling on blue surgical gloves, Gregg and Jeremy started their examination. Habib, his face covered by a scarf to conceal his identity, stood nearby and translated. Taliban fighters often threatened Afghans working with American units. Habib didn't want to put himself or his family in danger.

"Is he in a lot of pain generally?" Gregg asked the boy's father.

"When he breathes," the man said. The boy—named Agha Wali—stood still and smiled.

"Can he take his shirt off?" Gregg asked as he threaded his stethoscope through his fingers. "He has trouble breathing, Habib? All the time?"

With his shirt off, the bow in the boy's back looked even worse. He was skinny and you could see his ribs.

"It is always the same," the father said. "It doesn't' get worse. It is always the same. Day and night."

Putting the stethoscope on the boy, Gregg started to listen to his lungs. Sliding the stethoscope around the boy's chest, he asked him to breathe deeply.

"He's not bringing up any fluid? Does he wake up real sweaty?" Gregg asked.

Nearby, Jeremy started to flip through a small medical book with a yellow cover.

Done with his chest, Gregg had the boy turn around so that he could put the stethoscope to his back. With each deep breath, Gregg told the boy "good job." When he was finished examining him, he told the boy to put his shirt on and turned to Jeremy.

"I'm not hearing any fluid. That's good," Gregg said. "He's not having any night sweats or coughing up any lung butter. TB is not a big concern. I think what he is suffering from is respiratory distress because of how much spinal deformation he has."

Jeremy suggested that they bring the boy to the camp for X-rays. Later, Jeremy did some research and ruled out spina bifida because there was no visible abnormality on the lumbar spine. It was Pott's disease, which is when tuberculosis is in the bones instead of the spine. Either way, the medics didn't have medication to treat the disorder.

Gregg told the boy's father to come up to Wilson to get the X-rays and to let doctors at the base examine him. Fishing out a bag of vitamins, he handed them to the boy's father.

"Just chew them up and eat them," Gregg said.

"It tastes good, right?" the father said.

"Yeah. They'll love them," Gregg said. "You'll have ten days' worth. Bring him by, and we'll make sure he gets more."

The clinic so far was pretty pointless. Many of the problems Gregg and Jeremy saw were well beyond their ability to treat from a backpack. A baby with birth defects was brought to them. So were several adults with minor aches and pains. I'd been to several of these clinics and it never failed that several Afghans showed up and complained of stomachaches or just aches in general. In these cases, a little bag of over-the-counter painkillers usually did the trick.

But the real aim here, and at most clinics, was intelligence gathering. There was always the chance that one of the patients who was seen would have some information. Maybe the location of a weapons cache or the location of a Taliban cell leader.

This time, though, there was nothing. Pretty much all Gregg and Jeremy got were patients with ailments they couldn't treat plus one drug addict. He came up toward the end of the hour-long clinic and asked Gregg for help. By this point, the medics had handed out pairs of blue gloves to the kids, who were having a fine old time blowing them up like balloons.

Sitting on the edge of the blanket, the man told Gregg he'd quit taking opium but needed drugs to help keep him off.

"Do you have a pill that I can take that will make me stop?" the man said.

Gregg shook his head and for the next several minutes tried to explain that the only way to treat addiction was through aggressive treatment.

"For opium addiction, it is methadone, which is also a controlled med which we don't have. If you want help with this thing, you're going to have to go to the hospital," Gregg said. "If you go to the hospital in Kandahar, they might have outpatient care. If you stop the drugs, you could suffer some withdrawal that can have some serious medical consequences. They will keep you locked down so that when you go through that withdrawal you can't go out looking for drugs."

The man wasn't hearing that. He wanted a magic pill.

"I told you that I've decided to quit," the addict said. "If I stay here, can you give me something so that I am not forced to go all the way to Kandahar?"

"Unfortunately I can't," Gregg said. "That's what you're going to have to do if you want to quit. It's a strong drug. You know that. Because it is such a strong drug, there is no easy solution."

I'd seen people like this addict in the past, in Iraq, Kenya, and other villages in Afghanistan. It was easy to understand where they were coming from really. We were Americans. We'd put people on the moon. So why didn't we have a pill that cures, well, everything?

I'd actually heard an Iraqi ask that very question. He wanted to know how the United States could master space travel but couldn't fix the electric power in Baghdad.

CHAPTER 23

BEST CHICKEN IN AFGHANISTAN

The night in Afghanistan was suffocating.

With no ambient light, life came to a halt when the sun set. And darkness came quickly. The sun started to race to the horizon around 5 P.M., and within what seemed like minutes it was too dark to see.

We were sitting next to one of the checkpoints near Highway One. We'd come to patrol a village just south of the road. The ANCOP had gotten a tip that the Taliban was setting up checkpoints on the dirt roads behind a thicket of trees. A few villagers had come up and reported the checkpoint. So, hoping to catch them in the act, the team set up a patrol to root them out.

But the patrol was a bust.

We'd gotten there a few hours before dusk. It took us several minutes to get organized. The new dog handler had arrived and this was one of his first missions. It's never easy being the new guy and the team was riding him from the minute he arrived.

The new dog handler, Greg, who spelled his name with only one *g* at the end, was an MP from the Old Guard, the unit responsible for guarding the Tomb of the Unknown Soldier in Arlington National Cemetery. Besides being in charge of ceremonial duties, the Old Guard had deployed dog teams and other specialty units.

Compared to their predecessors, Jake and Apollo, Greg and his dog, Gerko, were a huge step down. Meek and with a stubby tail that had been amputated because he kept biting it, the dog acted old and uninterested. I first saw him in the camp when Greg was taking him to the far corner to defecate. When he squatted, Gerko began shaking like he was shitting tacks. It was painful to watch.

It seemed like all the dog did was crap. After we got out of the truck, Courtney told Greg to search for an IED near a bridge in the area; a few minutes later, Greg and the dog were approaching the bridge, getting ready to search it, and suddenly there was Gerko, once again assuming shitting posture.

During the patrol, Greg and the dog were supposed to stay close to Matt, but the dog's bowel movements kept messing this up, and Matt kept ending up well ahead of him. As we approached the village, Greg became flustered when some sheep passed.

"You better get those sheep away from my dog," he said.

I felt bad for the kid.

We snaked our way into the village. There were only two families living in the cluster of compounds in the village of Haji Makhadem and they told the team that the Taliban had moved south, despite reports that a machine-gun team had been shooting at a convoy on the highway that afternoon.

For the most part, the village was deserted. The guns at Camp Wilson had bombed some of the compounds out. The ANCOP, maybe sensing the lack of danger, strolled more than patrolled and didn't seem engaged in the mission.

Several times, Courtney or Matt had to yell at them to pay attention, pull security, or generally move with a purpose. After an hour of patrolling, Courtney decided to return to the checkpoint on Highway One. The plan was to wait there until dark and then set up observation points near the canal.

After setting up the trucks along the perimeter, Courtney, Rick, and I went into the shipping-container-turned-break-room and we sat down with our backs against the western wall to have dinner.

The walls of the checkpoints were built around the container with a tower perched on its roof. A machine gunner watched the highway from the tower. Hesco barriers filled with dirt, and concertina wire, protected the checkpoint from attack. Power came from a gas-powered generator and meals were cooked in a small kitchen, covered by a plywood roof, in the corner of the Hesco-barrier wall.

Inside the container, the ANCOP had built a small platform in the back where they could sit and sleep. A mat covered the floor and pillows lined the walls. At a glance, it looked like a typical Afghan living room. When we got there, many of the ANCOP were huddled on the mat eating dinner. Shoes were piled up by the door. Kicking off our boots, we joined them.

Still wearing our body armor, we moved like fat people with little arms. Unable to reach the food placed on the mat, we had to lean over at the waist.

It was a lot of work, but it was worth it.

The chicken, perfectly cooked and served in metal bowls that held the juices, practically melted in my mouth. Coupled with bread, moist rice, and fresh tomatoes, it was one of the best meals I'd had in weeks. Far better than the food at the dining hall at Wilson.

After taking several bits of chicken and scoops of rice, Courtney said what we were all thinking.

"This is the best chicken I've had and I got it in a checkpoint off of Highway One."

Next came steaming-hot chai with milk. It was sweet and the milk was creamy. Courtney preferred milk chai to the regular, more watery version. For me, I couldn't stomach the milky "skin" that formed over the top of the chai. It was nasty and I sucked my tea down quickly in an attempt to keep the milk from congealing.

Putting my empty glass on the tray, I waddled out so that Jeremy could come in and get some food. Standing outside, I looked up at the stars. With no light pollution from the city, the sky was a tapestry of light. More stars than I'd ever seen.

Leaning against the door, I listened to Rick talk to the Afghans about home.

"So, do you guys have any plans for your leave time?" he asked.

The ANCOP guys were rotating back to Herāt in a few weeks. Like them, I was headed home too. I hadn't really thought about my return. Running my hand over my cheek, I noticed that my beard was huge. Thick, with more gray than I'd remembered from other trips. My body armor was laden with a first-aid kit, an equipment pouch, and a holster for a radio. I was starting to look like the guys I had seen on the Shadow flight I'd arrived on.

Back inside the container, the Afghans talked about going home to their families, about parties and marriages. Many of the men were getting married. Even Joker had told me about his impending marriage.

Rick, whose wife was expecting a child, told the Afghans that he was sure it was a boy.

"I used a different position," he said.

The joke produced a hearty laugh.

Going back to the truck, I met up with Ben and Matt. Standing around waiting, we all knew that there was no way we'd see any Taliban tonight. The enemy had been reduced to rumors or ghosts. And with only a few weeks to go, I was pretty sure we'd never catch them. It is strange to hope for action when what you're hoping for could be deadly. In your head, you only imagine victory and heroics. But in reality, action could mean an IED that killed or maimed one of the team or even you yourself.

On the more than dozen embeds I'd been on, I'd never chased action. It wasn't healthy. But I'd be lying if I said deep down I wasn't hoping that we'd catch some Taliban before I had to leave Afghanistan. If for no other reason than to use some of the ammo that I'd been dragging around for weeks. It would be nice, for once, to go on patrol and be able to walk back with a lighter load.

The rest of the mission that night we spent sitting around the trucks watching the tree line. The team took turns on the truck's main gun, using the camera and night-vision sights to scan the trees and compounds nearby.

Ben saw a motorcycle stirring up a dust cloud miles away from the village, but couldn't make out any weapons. The only confirmed living creature was a massive Afghan dog. Matt spotted it as we drove back to Wilson. Its head reached to about a man's chest. In the infra-red camera, you could just make out its shaggy coat.

"It is huge, bro," Matt said as he looked into the monitor. "It looks like two Taliban dressed like a dog."

CHAPTER 24

CONTACT

Moments after we pulled into Pulchakhan, an RPG round exploded nearby.

I heard the boom just as I climbed out of the truck.

Instantly, the ANCOP soldiers in the nearest tower started shooting at two guys in black with a PKM machine gun. They fired from the hip, the rounds arcing into the air over the heads of soldiers in an American convoy driving by.

Standing next to the truck, I saw Matt race into the guard tower. Gregg and Mike the Cop were close behind. The radio in my headphones crackled to life as Matt saw the guys running away. They were posing as sheepherders, except one was carrying an RPG round in a green canvas backpack. Once the ANCOP started shooting, the two Taliban fighters dumped the round and hid behind a tree, I heard Matt say.

"Cap, this is Matt. At the far tree line there are two guys in black man-jams. They are right in front of that wall running north–south. How copy?"

Matt picked up his rifle and trained it on the fighters. The tower was crowded with ANCOP. Some were on guard. Others were up there to see the action. Nearby, Habib waited to translate Matt's commands. Standing in front of Matt was Gregg, pressed against the side of the tower, scanning the wall for the two men in man-jams.

"You see them?" Matt said to Gregg.

In the distance, another RPG round exploded.

"There it is," Matt said. "That's another RPG blast right there."

Matt had them in his sights first. Slowly sliding his finger to the trigger, he fired. The shot took Gregg by surprise. He'd been focused on his scope, searching for a target, and looked up, confused.

"He's standing still. The bad guy, right?" said Mike the Cop. He was set up inside the tower trying to help the ANCOP machine gunners.

"I see them now, dude," Gregg said, finally catching a glimpse of the fighters squatting near the wall.

"Yeah, you see them," Matt said.

"Are we clear to engage them?" Gregg asked.

Matt said yes, and less than a second later, Gregg was firing. He got off two shots before Matt told him he was short. Matt and Gregg took turns firing at the men, trying to arc the bullets to the target. Finally, some of Gregg's shots hit near one of the fighters, who ducked behind the wall.

"There you go," Matt said. "Now he is moving."

"He's by that wall, right?" Gregg said.

"Yup. Behind that wall," Matt said.

They both took two more shots that missed.

"Okay, cease," Matt said, raising his rifle up to the sky and keying his radio. "This is Matty. Go ahead."

"Do you want the PKM gunner to shoot at the men since the machine gun has greater range?" Mike the Cop asked.

But after the ANCOP'S first burst, which sent a stream of rounds into the sky, over a U.S. convoy no less, Matt nixed the idea.

"They can't hit shit," Matt yelled back into the guard tower before going back to talking to the captain on the radio.

"Roger that. Our guy has taken a knee. He is behind a wall approximately five hundred meters away. How copy?"

Near the tower, Courtney and the others tried to get the ANCOP ready to move. Despite all the shooting that was going on, the ANCOP weren't ready to patrol. They were still pulling out machine-gun ammunition from cans and putting on their equipment. The team quickly herded them into the three squads, yelling at them to hurry up.

Matt climbed down from the tower and led the first group out of the gate. Gregg and Mike the Cop stayed and provided cover.

Falling in behind Josh and Rick, I followed the rest of the team out of the gate. We cut through a graveyard on the side of the road. In the distance, you could hear gunfire. It started as a few rifle shots, followed by machine-gun fire. I could hear jets roaring overhead. As we walked closer, another RPG exploded.

"Oh shit," Josh said in his southern twang. "I hear RPGs."

"They're trying to get away from us," John said.

The team and ANCOP were spread out in three wedges. We weaved in and out of the graves as we walked. Some of the guys just walked over the pile of rocks, but John made sure he gave each stone a wide berth.

"I don't want to step on these graves," he said when Josh asked him what he was doing.

Past the graveyard, the team and ANCOP tore across a plowed field toward the sound of the guns. Carrying six magazines and two frags on my back, I didn't feel the weight at all as we ran through the field and a canal. My shoulders didn't burn and all I could focus on were the guns.

They'd start and stop like an old car struggling not to stall. It felt like the guns were almost calling us to hurry up. To get to the action.

"Be careful where you step," the captain warned us.

We were moving fast. I tried to look where I was stepping, but every time I did, I fell behind a step. Finally, I figured it was better to stay with the group than fall behind and slow them down.

Up ahead, there was a large mud compound with biscuit-colored walls. Matt and his squad of ANCOP soldiers, along with Tron and Mike, stopped to search it. Suddenly there was a massive explosion and a huge dark mushroom cloud rose up into the sky.

"Boom," Josh said as we started to run toward the tree line.

The smoke cloud crawled high into the sky. Likely it was an artillery round shot from Wilson. I followed Josh, Tony, and Rick as they pushed their ANCOP to the south around the compound and up a road that ran parallel to a dry wadi.

Shots rang out. An ANCOP was firing over a wall.

"Where are they at? Where are they at?" Josh yelled as the Afghan opened up with another burst. "I don't see shit. What are they shooting at?"

Rick, Josh, and Tony were already lined up along the same mud wall, aiming at a cluster of compounds separated by a field. The ANCOP commander came up and pointed across the field.

"The wall? The wall?" Josh said.

The Afghan again opened fire at what looked like just a wall. Josh slowly made his way down the wall behind the commander, trying to see the ANCOP guys' target. I kept close behind Josh, keeping my head down and only peeking up occasionally with my video camera to see if I could identify what the ANCOP were spraying with bullets.

"Where are they at?" Rick asked as Josh passed.

"I don't see shit, man," Josh said, peeking over the wall again.

After the last burst, we held that position for a few more seconds before catching up with the ANCOP, who were already moving down the road. There was a manic feeling in the air as the team tried to track down the men who had fired the RPG. But moving that fast was a good way to blunder into an IED. Courtney finally slowed the patrol down after Tron found a few military-age males and started questioning them in the compound.

Standing on the bank of the canal, Josh and I could hear the pop of rifle rounds and the *rat-tat-tat* of the machine guns in the distance. Josh kept looking toward the gunfire. It seemed to pull him.

"Let's keep pushing," he said, more to himself, it seemed, than to anyone else.

Pushing up into a cluster of compounds, the team stopped to search them. As we stood on the corner near the first compound, the village elder came out to meet us. Rick told him to stop and the ANCOP quickly searched him.

The elder, whose name was Pir Mohammed, had a hawklike nose, dark eyes, and his skin looked like he spent hours in the sun. He told the ANCOP that four days ago, the Taliban had come to the village and roughed up the mullah. The Taliban fighters told the villagers to stay inside and to not go down to their fields south of the village.

"Where did they go?" Rick asked.

"They travel the main road on motorcycles," the elder said in Pashto. Rza, standing nearby, translated.

Soon we saw two men on a red motorcycle coming down the road. The ANCOP stopped them. Pulling them off the bike, they marched them over to Rick, who separated them. One sat near the door to the elder's compound. The other sat facing the wall around the corner, looking sullen. Rick called Courtney over to question them.

Both Afghan men had dark beards and trimmed mustaches. They wore dark *shalwar kameez* man-jams and vests. Henna stained their nails and palms and both wore eyeliner. They seemed puzzled about why they'd been stopped. Sitting down on top of a low mud wall, Courtney leaned into the first man.

Rza stood nearby, ready to translate.

"He better tell me where he is coming from," Courtney said in a very even tone.

The man said something in Pashto and Rza translated.

"He says they came from up north and they are going home."

"Don't play stupid with me. You came from the east. Where is your fucking weapon?" Courtney said.

The Afghan said he didn't have a weapon. He was a farmer. Nothing more.

"You know why you came from there. You were fucking over there shooting U.S. personnel," Courtney said.

The man insisted he wasn't doing that, saying that he came from the north, not from the east where the firefight had broken out.

"You can't hear the firefight? Is the Taliban down there?" Courtney said.

"No."

"How about to the east?" Courtney asked.

"No."

Courtney was frustrated. Standing there watching the questioning, I understood why soldiers talk about wanting to take suspected fighters' heads and smash them into the wall. I had no idea if this guy had come from the firefight or not, but everything pointed to his story being a lie.

"It is kind of ironic that he is coming over here on a motorcycle," Courtney said. "Tell him I don't believe him."

While the captain talked to the other man, and got virtually the same story, I tried to figure out why I was feeling some of the same frustration as Courtney. I wasn't really in any danger, especially not from the guys on the motorcycle. I hadn't been shot at, and yet I was convinced that these men were Taliban. I was certain they'd been out shooting at Americans, and if they'd had the opportunity, they would have shot at us. They had simply stumbled into the patrol and had luckily had enough time to ditch their weapons before they were apprehended.

By now, the shooting had stopped and kids started to come out of the village asking for pens, water, and candy. One kid was making donkey noises as he ran down the road toward the patrol. He was cradling a white toy truck in his arms. Josh tried to talk with him and even played a little bit with the truck. When Josh took it, the boy got all nervous and kissed Josh's hand when he returned it.

I was giving Jolly Ranchers to the kids when the boy came up and started whimpering like a dog. After I gave him a piece of candy, he ran off into a nearby field and started running in circles, clutching his truck.

Some of the ANCOP stopped to watch, but most ignored him. I couldn't stop watching him. He was oblivious to the war around him. For him the sound of gunfire and the machines of war that rumbled up the road around the village meant nothing. He was content with his truck, some candy, and a spin through the fields.

Josh came up to inform us that the kid probably wasn't the village idiot he seemed to be.

"He's really a spotter for the Taliban," Josh said. "He's really a genius."

While the two suspected fighters sat there waiting, Courtney met with the village elder. Pir Mohammed greeted him warmly and seemed eager to help.

"Those two individuals that we have detained on the other side of the village, do you know them?" Courtney asked.

While Courtney talked on the radio to Matt, who was still with

Tron in a nearby compound, Rza translated. Pir Mohammed spoke rapidly and pointed with a flat palm toward a cluster of compounds in the south.

"They know those guys. They know where they are from," Rza said. "They are good people. They are not TBs."

"So the guys that we got are actually good guys?" Courtney asked. "Where are they from?"

Pir Mohammed again pointed to a village to the south.

"They are farmers," the elder said.

But the Taliban had been in the village recently, he said.

"Did they have weapons?"

"No. Just radios, no weapons. They were just talking," the elder said.

"What were they saying?"

"They were just saying names," the elder said as Rza translated.

"Do you remember any of the names?"

"No. I don't remember."

"Where do they come from?"

"They come from all over. They set up a machine gun in a clump of trees and fired at convoys on Highway One," the elder said. "We can say nothing because they will beat us. They say this is none of our business."

Courtney walked back to where the men were sitting and let them go, but kept a cell phone he'd confiscated from one of them. The firefight was long over and the team was no closer to finding the Taliban. At least now they knew that they were in a village farther south and had been coming up to shoot at convoys.

After rounding up the ANCOP, we walked back to Pulchakhan. While we were gone, Gregg and Mike the Cop caught a man wearing a black *shalwar kameez* near the base. When they tested his hands for explosives, he came up positive.

Rick, Tron, and Courtney questioned him for an hour or so at Pulchakhan. While we waited, Matt gave the ANCOP a pep talk. They'd performed poorly and he wanted to make sure they understood that this wasn't acceptable. There had been no sense of urgency during the patrol and they had quickly become bored and weren't keeping watch after the shooting stopped.

"Translate exactly what I say," Matt said to Habib through clenched teeth.

Matt called the ANCOP together and made them huddle close.

"What the fuck is going on? You think this is a goddamn picnic? We can't go get in a gunfight because we are too busy herding you guys," Matt said. "You guys are out there swinging your rifles, drinking tea, and sitting down. If I see one more goddamn camera, I am going to shove it up that guy's ass. You guys are better than this. During the first patrol, you were money. What is the deal, guys?"

Most of the ANCOP just stood there stone-faced. They were embarrassed. Gregg yelled at two Afghans who were smiling, but most of them understood the message. When Matt was done, the captain spoke to them. The ANCOP only had a few weeks left before they returned to Herāt, and Courtney wanted to make sure they understood the message.

"Unless you guys want to go home in a body bag, you better start listening to my guy. Right now you look like sheep out there. You need to look like wolves every time you go out on patrol," the captain said. "There are guys out there that want to kill you. I refuse to go out there and get one of my guys killed."

CHAPTER 25

ARMAGEDDON HARD-ON

It was the team's fifth mission in ten weeks.

With about two weeks to go before the end of my embed, the team was given a new mission. They'd been tapped to leave Zhari and head down to the Horn of Panjwai to take over a VSO site. The battalion planned to put three teams in the area before the following year's fighting season.

Major Haskell, the B-team commander, came down to Wilson a few days after the team received the news about the mission; the major and company were to escort the team to a meeting with Haji Baran Khaksar, district governor of Panjwai. They wanted the governor's input on where to put the teams. The idea was to connect the teams up with influential leaders in the district and let them win over the people.

Packed into the back of Matt's truck, I watched as we crossed from Zhari into Panjwai. As we snaked our way through a market, teeming with men, women, and children shopping, it looked nothing like the Panjwai I'd written about in a previous book.

That book was about how a small group of Special Forces soldiers and their Afghan partners took the Horn from the Taliban in a massive battle in 2006. The fight, over a small hill not far from the district center, changed the way the Taliban conducted themselves in battle. Instead of trying to fight toe-to-toe with U.S. forces, they'd started building roadside bombs, recruited suicide bombers from Pakistan, and blended into the population. This put a serious dent in the United States' ability to conduct air strikes. Civilian casualties were to be avoided. The Taliban knew it. So did the United States. By keeping close to women and kids, the Taliban was able to keep the air cover away.

But the Panjwai I was now seeing was different. The market was vibrant. The stores were well stocked and boys in school uniforms darted in and out of the storefronts. It wasn't a war zone anymore, or at least it wasn't at this market.

There was still trouble along the goat paths and in the tangle of dry wadis and thick fields that made up most of the Horn. This was Taliban land, much like Zhari, and by laying claim to it, the Coalition was making a statement. They were going to take away the Taliban's home field.

"Every time we've gone into the Horn of Panjwai, we've left," Haskell told me at the Panjwai district headquarters. "They don't think we'll stay. This is why there's a big push to get down there."

Reaching the end of the market, we turned into the district governor's compound. Parking near the tent city where a 20th Special Forces Group team was living with their own ANCOP, we all got out of the trucks. As we stood in the gravel parking lot, the mountains towered all around us high above the base. They looked massive, almost fake, like a painting on a Hollywood set. It was the same set of mountains I'd watch the sun peek over from the other side in Zhari.

Before going to meet Haji Baran, Courtney and other team leaders and sergeants met with Haskell in a makeshift team room. While members of the 20th SF Group lounged on couches or foldout chairs, Haskell stood in front of the group and introduced Courtney. He told them how the Courtney team had been "jerked around" more than any other team in Afghanistan.

But this would be the team's final mission.

The new plan called for the team to set up a VSO site in Taloqan. A group from 3rd Group would set up in Mushan and a 20th Group team would set up in Zangabad. By the time I left, that plan had changed several times, with the captain and his team taking over the site in Zangabad.

But first everyone had to go to meet Haji Baran.

His office was across the camp from the 20th Group's base. It was a cavernous room with vinyl chairs, ornately patterned carpets, and glass tables. The more than a dozen Americans and their interpreters filed in, sitting on opposite sides of the table.

Baran, dressed in a dark turban and gray *shalwar kameez,* sat in a swivel chair in front of his desk. The first thing I noticed was the large scar on his forehead. He was a big man and spoke in a deep voice. It was like he'd been plucked from central casting.

District governors in Afghanistan are not elected officials. They are appointed by the central government in Kabul. Baran was part of the Noorzai tribe, which dominated the district. The tribe was known to be pro-Taliban, which was why Panjwai had been a haven for fighters. It had been a safe haven for the mujahideen during the Soviet invasion as well.

The governor apologized for failing to have dinner for his guests and for his ability to offer only tea, sweets, and some pistachios and other nuts. Baran praised Captain Rick, the 20th Group Team leader, for all his work in the region and told Haskell that he should promote him. Rick had been working closely with the elder for weeks, and being so close they'd forged a bond.

Haskell told him that the other team leaders who were headed to the district were as competent as Rick and then laid out the plan to bring three teams into the Horn and set up in the village.

"We are coming here for advice. The soldiers from the 101st in Mushan, Taloqan, and Zangabad are going to leave. They are going to be replaced by three Special Forces teams. The intent is for them to go in and stay," Haskell explained. "We are going to need some strong, brave men to help and we are going to need some help finding a place for them to go."

The governor liked the plan, but requested that the team leaders meet with him to talk about their plans before they put them into effect.

"We have to follow the religious way and the Pashtun way," he said.

He said that the teams should come with a big force because the Soviets came in with three thousand men and still failed. Zangabad, he said, was the "stronghold of the enemy." The governor said if you send one hundred soldiers into Mushan, you need to send two hundred to Zangabad. He said that there were now about two thousand families in Zangabad, but that in the past there had been six thousand. Most of them had moved to Kandahar City because of the fighting in the area.

"Will the families come back if there is security?" Haskell asked.

"They don't like life in the city," the governor said. "The Taliban come and beat them in the head and the government beats them on the other side of the head."

Haskell said that his men planned to hire locals to build the camps.

"The people are desperate to work," the governor said. "People will come back to work if there is security. The Taliban said the Coalition is going to go to their houses and destroy them. So, coming back and bringing security will assure the people that they can come back and work the land."

"We want to make sure we're hiring the right people," Haskell said. "We're going to need your help."

The governor said if the teams wanted to help, then they needed to make sure they talked with the shura, a body of elders authorized to make decisions for the village or tribe. If you have to pay for damages, then do it in front of the shura. Afghans rarely believe something they can't see. But while he approved of the plans, he said that none of them mattered now. Baran told them that plans didn't mean anything in the winter. Control the area for one day in the spring, he said.

"If you are still standing in the spring, they will give you credit," he said.

"We will be there in the spring," Haskell said.

A few days later, Courtney, Tron, and I flew out to Mushan to check out the town. We went to a shura, which was widely attended, and ate lunch with some locals before taking a helicopter back to the district center. At that time, the team was slated to be stationed in Mushan. But a few days later, they were switched to the Zangabad mission.

The mission kept changing, which was one of the reasons I decided not to prolong my stay. I'd seen how quickly plans changed and there was talk that the 101st was going to push to keep the team in Zhari. It turned out that they didn't do this, but I'd seen time lines change too often, and I didn't really want to have to watch the team build another camp, even if it gave me a chance to cover the Village Stability mission.

Plus, Colonel Agha and his men were rotating back to Herāt. So, it seemed like a fitting time to leave. On my last patrol in Zhari, I tried to take in as much of Afghanistan as I could. It was late in the afternoon when we arrived in Pulchakhan. The team planned to visit the village where they'd chased the Taliban fighters a few days before and then wait until after a massive bombardment to patrol the village near the ruins.

The 101st, which was still pushing south, was going to conduct a massive air strike on the ruins as a show of force. John got the details and it promised to be a spectacular show. But first we had to patrol. It was an uneventful slog through the fields and wadis. At one point, Courtney stopped to talk with some elders again. While they talked, Rick asked me to try to get a picture of one of the elders.

Maneuvering in front of him, I aimed my camera. He saw me and dodged out of the way. I grabbed Rick and Josh, and we did an impromptu photo shoot. I angled each shot in order to get the elder in the frame, finally snapping several usable mug shots.

On the way back, I found myself next to Rza. He was ranting about the Taliban and how they were destroying the area. The Taliban fighters were not good Muslims, he said.

"Why not?" I asked as we crossed the last wadi and started across the fields toward Pulchakhan.

"Because they are not following the Muslim rules. The Muslim rules, you can't give a hard time to the people. You have to give freedom. You have to give them what they want. What they choose," he said. "You can't play a game with the people's future. These people, they are playing a game with their kids' future. They choose for them what they have to be. And the second thing you can't do, you can't ever be lying in Islam. But they are always lying."

As a Hazara, Rza had a special hatred for the Taliban and for Pashtuns as well. The Hazara suffered large ethnic massacres, carried out by the predominately ethnic Pashtun Taliban, in the late 1990s. A Taliban saying about non-Pashtuns goes: "Tajiks to Tajikistan, Uzbeks to Uzbekistan, and Hazaras to *goristan*"—to the graveyard.

"Pashtuns always lie," Rza continued. "All the people do here is pray. Americans are better Muslims."

This was the kind of internal divisions a unified Afghanistan would have to bridge if it was ever to become a successful nation. For most of the trip, I'd watch the ANCOP soldiers work together. Men from different tribes and different areas. But I knew not to be fooled by the appearance of concord. The country still had to face serious problems with tribalism. It wasn't as bad as it had been in the past when ANA soldiers and ANCOP wouldn't even sleep in the same room with members of another tribe, but like with our own civil rights problems in the United States, the feelings weren't going to go away easily.

"If they win, they will kill the people. That is not Islam," Rza said. "I kill people while I work with Coalition forces. I have to protect my family. What should I do? I have to work."

Hating the Taliban, especially from a Hazara, wasn't news. But Rza's contempt for the Pashtuns in the village was almost as venomous as his contempt for the Taliban.

"These people don't have any knowledge of Islam. They are just following what they heard," Rza said. "They don't know exactly what they are supposed to do. Fucking just praying is not good enough, bro."

That night, we gathered up on the wall to watch the show. It was pitch-black and I could barely see a few feet beyond the wall that surrounded the compound. Blowing air into my hands to keep warm, I squinted in the direction of the ruins. Nearby, John was on the radio.

I could faintly hear the voices of the pilots, circling high above, preparing for the strike.

"That is probably the fighter right there moving to the east," John said. I could barely see the F-15. It looked like a fast-moving star and was hard to pick out in the tapestry of other stars in the sky.

The strike was going to be massive. F-15 fighters and B-1 bombers dropping thousands of pounds of explosives on the ruined mud huts nearby.

"Six seconds," John said.

I saw the flash first.

The pitch-black farmland around us suddenly burst into light as a massive mushroom cloud formed where the bombs had hit. Seconds later, the roar of the blast washed over us like a wave. I could hear Matt laughing as the bombs hit and the fire shot high into the sky.

"I've got an Armageddon hard-on after that," John said. "The explosion just sat there and I am like whacking off to it. Yeah. Yeah."

Then out of the darkness we heard the whistling of a piece of shrapnel. It landed with a *thunk* against the Hesco wall in front of us. The sound was sickening and I could only imagine what it would have been like if it had hit one of us.

"That was close as fuck," John commented.

Retreating to a spot behind the wall, he said that what we'd seen were six five-hundred-pound bombs. The pilots still had more five-hundreds and eight two-thousand-pound bombs. The second round was going to be bigger than the first.

The second flash again came before the boom, but this boom was different. This one seemed to rumble from the core of the earth. It reminded me of the aftershocks I'd felt when I was covering the earthquake in Haiti. These bombs had an almost primal roar. It was the most violent thing I'd ever seen. It was spectacular in a very scary way. I couldn't imagine being the target of a U.S. Air Force strike.

With each strike, there was more cheering. It is impossible to watch explosions with a group of soldiers without hearing the cheers. Even during a firefight, there'd be cheers. People just seem to naturally yell out when the bombs start hitting.

This night was no different. Afterward, we all were sort of in awe.

"There's nothing left," Matt said. "They bombed the dog shit out of that place."

"The villagers are going to think the end of the world just came," Courtney said.

"And next time we go down south, it will be 'hey, they got a new lake,'" Tony quipped.

I never got to see that new lake. This was my final mission.

EPILOGUE

The day I left, the ANCOP left as well. With all of them lined up for a final formation, several were awarded medals before being released. Running to their trucks, the ANCOP were excited to drive back to Herāt. As Colonel Agha and his officers departed, they shook hands with the team members and hugged them.

With that chapter closed, Courtney started to plan for the move to Panjwai. As for me, I threw my bags into the back of one of Colonel Riga's trucks and caught a ride back to Kandahar. I'd been invited to accompany Colonel Bolduc on a battlefield circulation. And when the commander of the Combined Joint Special Operations Task Force extends an invitation, everyone considers it an order.

Before I left, I watched the ANCOP leave. I knew the officers and recognized some of the men. But I really didn't know any of them. I'd made small talk with them at the checkpoints or around the camp. We all used to wave to one another at Camp Wilson. But even though our camps were side by side, I realized I'd failed to get to know any of the

Afghans. Part of it was a result of our different languages. I didn't know how to speak Dari and I didn't have a dedicated interpreter to help bridge the gap. The few times I did get to speak with any of them, like the one time I spoke to Joker, it didn't amount to much.

The gap was too big. Their worldview was too foreign to me and I truly didn't understand the roots of the tribal and ethnic problems that plagued Afghanistan. I understood the gist of the situation, but in order to change the way a nation and a people feel, a deeper level of understanding than I possessed was needed. So, as the ANCOP drove off, I realized that I didn't have that understanding of Afghanistan, and to be honest, I'm skeptical of any Westerner who says he does.

My final few days at Kandahar Airfield were dull. I did lots of reading, running, and writing. The one highlight was the battlefield circulation I accompanied Bolduc and Riga on. We flew around Kandahar Province in a Black Hawk visiting teams in the different districts. It was eye-opening to see what other teams were doing and that the emphasis on Village Stability Operations was paying some dividends. At each stop on the circulation, Colonel Bolduc talked to the teams about the importance of their mission.

At the end of the circulation, I spoke to the colonel myself. I'd known him since the time I was writing my book on the battle in Panjwai, and he still had the same intensity that had impressed me earlier. He deeply believed that the war could be won by the Special Forces. Speaking to a team in the western portion of Kandahar Province, near the Pakistan border, he told them that Village Stability Operations was a tough mission. There was no effective governance, but what they were doing, much like the team I had been with, was critical, especially for the children of Afghanistan. He said that the Coalition's narrative was better than the Taliban's.

"What do they bring? Despair. We bring hope. We bring the hope of better security. We bring the hope of better infrastructure. Clinics. Roads. Bridges. Things that people need to make their lives better. Their children's lives better. We bring the hope of a better government. A government based on democratic principles and respectful of the Islamic religion," Bolduc said. "The Taliban is the exact opposite. They bring murder and intimidation. They threaten people to get them to do what they want them to do. They actually subjugate women. Keep them from participating in the culture. They threaten Islamic religion."

Before he left to return to Bagram, I sat down and talked to him about what I'd learned. He'd asked me to do this. Here is what I told him:

* SF was slowly losing its unconventional mind-set as it became more tied to firebases, large armored vehicles, and the comforts of home. More teams needed to be out in civilian clothes and soft-skin vehicles, focusing on ways to achieve results in an unconventional way. Too often, the teams were moving in large armored convoys. There was little interaction with the populace, and when it did happen, the Special Forces soldier seemed so alien that he might as well have just stepped out of a spaceship. With each new protective device or vehicle, the Green Berets became better and better trained infantrymen, but that wasn't the point. Special Forces is people-centric, and the reliance on armored trucks was making it harder for the soldiers to reach the people they were targeting. Commanders needed to push teams out of their comfort zones and force commanders on the conventional side to permit teams to do Special Forces stuff.

* That unconventional mind-set was being lost in part because Special Forces teams didn't have the independence they needed

to have in order to work effectively on the battlefield. By making them beholden to the conventional officers running the battle space, the teams were hampered and couldn't use the agility that they needed to have in order to do their mission. Teams needed independence in order to build sources, gather intelligence, and act by, with, and through their Afghan partners. As troop levels decreased, I suspected that Colonel Bolduc would see a push to free up teams and allow them to go back to the way they'd performed in the past, when they worked parallel to the conventional units in an area instead of underneath them. And that, in my opinion, would be a good thing because unconventional units needed unconventional leaders.

* Special Forces was the only unit that could handle both Village Stability Operations (VSO) and FID (training foreign troops). Conventional units lacked the maturity, organization, and patience to accomplish such a mission. The keys to SF success in these areas went back to the root of Special Forces: the individual soldier.

* Selection worked and was finding self-motivated, passionate, and dedicated soldiers who were type A go-getters who needed very little supervision. During my embed, I asked every SF guy the same question: did you think you'd be selected? All of them said yes. I think the first question selection needed to ask was if a candidate had any doubt he'd be selected. Anyone who replied yes could then be asked to leave.

* Village Stability Operations was looked at as a defensive mission, forcing teams to sit and wait to get attacked. The teams liked being out in the villages, but they wanted the ability to be proactive and be able to seek out targets as well. On the flip side, the

downfall of the current Green Beret was the need and desire to perform raids. Few Green Berets I spoke to wanted to stay in Special Forces. Most wanted to migrate over to units, like Delta Force, that focused on raids and assaults. What was being lost was a Green Beret's passion for missions other than those involving combat. And with that loss, the Green Beret's unconventional mind-set was lost as well. Commanders had to get back to what made Special Forces special, and gunplay was not it.

* The ANCOP training mission was an essential Special Forces mission for two reasons. (1) No other force possessed the ability to train foreign troops as well. (2) ANCOP was a national asset directly linked to local governance, and the ANCOP were an ideal fit for the VSO mission because they were a positive example of the Afghan government in action. To a crafty and forward-thinking Special Forces commander, this kind of mission gave a team the most flexibility. ANCOP could perform numerous missions that could turn into big gains when the Afghans were paired with a team's intelligence network. What was stopping a team commander from doing a presence patrol in the area of a known enemy compound? The ANCOP could show the population that they were proactive not only in keeping the community safe, but in ferreting out the bad guys. A team commander wouldn't need to go through the longer operations planning process necessary for teams to deploy with commandos, nor would he need to beg for additional assets. An active team working its sources and the ANCOP's could have a larger impact on the battlefield than almost any other partnered unit.

One additional capability might be the creation of a SWAT-like force created and trained by the ODA. Based on Iraq's counterterrorism force, this small cadre of police could be used to hit targets and circumvent the longer mission approval process necessary to use commandos.

Bolduc seized upon what I said about village stability being seen as a defensive mission and said that he'd change his guidance to dispel that myth. To him, it was an offensive mission. It was the ultimate way to break up the insurgency and it would allow the Afghans to build up sufficient strength to win the war on their own.

"We're not going to shoot our way to victory," he said.

As I watched him leave our meeting, I realized I had only a few days left in Afghanistan. Going back to my room, I packed away my body armor for the trip home. Before I slid it into my green kit bag, I noticed how worn the straps had become. And there, in a pile, were several pouches for my gear and radio and a first-aid kit. When I looked in the mirror, I saw that my beard was a tangled mess and I noticed how tired I looked.

It had only been ten weeks. The guys, now headed to Panjwai, had months to go before they'd be home.

Boarding the charter to Dubai, I listened to contractors talk about trips to bars they had planned once they landed. They all seemed excited to be headed home or at least on leave. I wasn't ready to go home, despite a wife and son who missed me. I missed my family and not only had I missed most of the football season, but my middle brother got remarried while I was gone. But I felt guilty about leaving.

For the next several months, I kept in touch with some of the guys via e-mail. They'd send messages updating me on missions or on how things were going in the Horn. No one got killed. Matt did get hit by an IED, but fortunately he came away unscathed.

I didn't see much of the team once they got back to Fort Bragg. The 7th Special Forces Group was moving to Florida, and they had to pack and head south. Courtney, Tony, Josh, and Matt are all still on the team in Florida. So are Mike and Jeremy. Dave was reassigned to another unit. Gregg stayed at Fort Bragg. He was getting out of the Army and planned to enroll in medical school at the University of Wisconsin. Tron is working at the JFK Special Warfare Center and School. Rick left the team and is working at the battalion staff. Jake, the dog handler, was out of the Army briefly, but returned for his dog, Apollo. Both are still making trips to Afghanistan.

It was inevitable that we'd all go our separate ways after the deployment. It was part of the Army culture for the team members to move to other assignments and advance their careers. For me, I needed some distance to write because I'd become part of the story, if I wanted to or not. I knew the team I embedded with was gone as soon as I left and it was now my job to make sense of what I saw.

I set out to write a contemporary *Green Berets,* but left Afghanistan with a book that was closer to *Dispatches,* Michael Herr's memoir of his time as a correspondent for *Esquire* magazine during the Vietnam War—except without the violence and drugs. The book was less upbeat and gung-ho than Robin Moore's work.

It was a strange trip. In some ways, the lack of action was an asset. This could have easily been a book about the horrors of war, describing battle after battle. Instead, I was able to capture the daily slog of war in Afghanistan and hopefully offer readers a chance to see the obstacles soldiers face every day from an inaccessible Afghan culture to a bureaucratic system that takes the fight out of units.

The Gentlemen Bastards were in some ways the perfect team. They were young, motivated, and tried hard to do good. But they were up against obstacles that even the savviest commanders couldn't get around. Hamstrung by an ever-changing mission, which made it impossible to get much traction, the team did what it could when it could.

Did the ANCOP do good things? Yes. Did they have a major impact? No.

Some of the team complained that their talents were wasted on their deployment with ANCOP, but I'd argue that the Afghan police force will be better in the future and at least know what "right" looks like. That is a big step toward working the Special Forces out of a job.

I will always be grateful for the invitation to embed with the unit and for their generosity in allowing me a glimpse of life in Special Forces. It is a club where membership is earned and I was happy to get a temporary pass.

KEVIN MAURER is an award-winning reporter who has covered the military, with a focus on special operations forces, for eight years. He has been embedded with the U.S. Special Forces in Afghanistan, Iraq and Africa. He lives in Wilmington, North Carolina.